STEAM LOCOMOTIVE NICKNAMES

An illustrated dictionary from
Aberdare to Zeppelin

Thomas Middlemass

Silver Link Publishing Ltd

First published in November 1991

British Library Cataloguing in Publication Data

Middlemass, Thomas
Steam locomotive nicknames: an illustrated dictionary
from Aberdare to Zeppelin.
I. Title
625. 2610941

ISBN 0 947971 70 X

Silver Link Publishing Ltd
The Trundle
Ringstead Road
Great Addington
Kettering
Northamptonshire NN14 4BW

Typeset by G&M, Raunds, Northamptonshire
Printed in Great Britain by
Woolnough Bookbinding Limited, Irthlingborough, Northamptonshire,
and bound by The Bath Press, Bath

CONTENTS

INTRODUCTION

Some 15 years have elapsed since I consolidated my interest in the subject of locomotive nicknames by producing a modest booklet on the subject; and in that booklet I offered the following sentiments as an Introduction:

In human affairs nicknames are as old as life itself. Highly selective, and usually accurate, they have long been employed to convey affection (as in 'Lillibet'), resignation (as in 'Lofty') and sometimes plain perception (as in, let's face it, 'Stinker').

Exactly the same principle applies to steam locomotives, for no other 19th-century invention breached the human heart more securely. When a Scottish driver referred to his engine as a 'Wee Ben', and his southern counterpart bemoaned the fact that he was, once again, saddled with a 'Big Gobbler', we may be sure that relations between man and machine were warm, in more ways than one. Thus, over a century and more the majestic path of the steam locomotive acquired its rich underlay of nicknames. Love, hate, humour, testiness, inspiration, perspiration—all the emotions are there, and can be detected in the 250 nicknames we have listed for your inspection. Doubtless many more exist. We brace ourselves accordingly.

It was as well I *did* brace myself, for the booklet excited such interest that I received a positive shoal of letters from interested readers. Gentle corrections abounded. 'Dear Sir, surely you must be aware that Lanky tank engines were frequently referred to as "Yellow Bellies", and that their big 0-8-2 tanks were known as "Little Egberts"?' 'Dear Sir, when I worked at York shed in pre-war years Robinson's famous ROD 2-8-0s, with their draughty cabs, were still being dismissed by ex-North Eastern men as "Pneumonia Engines"...'

The sheer enthusiasm of this response so impressed me that I decided to mend my ways, and embark on a much closer inspection of the subject. The result is that in the following pages my total haul of locomotive nicknames has been increased to just over 450! Needless to say, I am duly grateful to my sundry mentors, and can only conclude by re-expressing the sentiments contained in the final paragraph of my original Introduction:

Sprung from a railway family himself, your author clings to a simple belief that men of steam were a great breed. He is, too, immodest enough to hope production of this book may shed a little more light towards understanding the kind of life they loved to lead.

Thomas Middlemass
Theydon Bois
Essex

LIST OF ABBREVIATIONS

B&ER	Bristol & Exeter Railway	M&GNJC/R	Midland & Great Northern Joint Committee/Railway
B&LR	Ballymena & Larne Railway		
B&NCR	Belfast & Northern Counties Railway	M&SWJR	Midland & South Western Junction Railway
BR	British Railways	MR	Midland Railway
CME	Chief Mechanical Engineer	MS&LR	Manchester, Sheffield & Lincolnshire Railway
CR	Caledonian Railway		
ECR	Eastern Counties Railway	NBR	North British Railway
EUR	Eastern Union Railway	NER	North Eastern Railway
FR	Furness Railway	NLR	North London Railway
G&SWR	Glasgow & South Western Railway	OW&WR	Oxford, Worcester & Wolverhampton Railway
GCR	Great Central Railway	P&TR	Pembroke & Tenby Railway
GER	Great Eastern Railway	PTR&D	Port Talbot Railway & Docks
GNR	Great Northern Railway	R&SBR	Rhondda & Swansea Bay Railway
GNSR	Great North of Scotland Railway		
GSR	Great Southern Railway of Ireland	S&DJR	Somerset & Dorset Joint Railway
		SE&CR	South Eastern & Chatham Railway
GWR	Great Western Railway		
H&BR	Hull & Barnsley Railway	SER	South Eastern Railway
HR	Highland Railway	SHT	Swansea Harbour Trust
K&ESR	Kent & East Sussex Railway	SM&AR	Swindon, Marlborough & Andover Railway
L&YR	Lancashire & Yorkshire Railway		
LB&SCR	London, Brighton & South Coast Railway	SR	Southern Railway
		WC&PR	Weston-super-Mare, Clevedon & Portishead Railway
LC&DR	London, Chatham & Dover Railway		
LD&ECR	Lancashire, Derby & East Coast Railway		
LMSR	London Midland & Scottish Railway	MT	Mixed traffic
		NBL	North British Locomotive Co
LNER	London & North Eastern Railway	WD	War Department
LNWR	London & North Western Railway	i/c	Inside cylinder(ed)
		o/c	Outside cylinder(ed)
LSWR	London & South Western Railway	3-cyl	Three-cylinder(ed)
		2-6-0T	2-6-0 side tank
LT&SR	London, Tilbury & Southend Railway	0-6-0ST	0-6-0 saddle tank
		2-4-0WT	2-4-0 well tank

THE DICTIONARY

'A' CLASS
See KNICK KNACKS.

ABBEY TANKS
See CORONATION TANKS.

ABERDARES
A Class of GWR i/c 2-6-0 with outside frames, of which the prototype, No 33, was built to William Dean's design in 1900. It was a neat and compact engine compared to its predecessor, the KRUGER (qv). Subject to some variation in detail, 80 more were built by 1907. Essentially freight engines, their nickname sprang from their original employment on heavy coal trains between Aberdare and Swindon. They remained on this traffic until well into the 1930s, when 20 of them were replaced by 2-8-0Ts. It was then that scrapping commenced, though one, No 2620, survived until August 1949. They were sturdy old engines, and 18 of those that continued in service throughout the Second World War notched up over one million miles each.

ABERDEENS
See GLASSHOUSES.

ADAMS'S FLYERS
LSWR Class 'T6' 4-4-0s, designed by William Adams, the construction of which commenced in June 1895. Ill health, however, forced Adams's retirement, and by the time the first of 10 appeared in September 1895 Dugald Drummond was in charge at Nine Elms. The first 'T6s' were employed straight away on express services between Waterloo and the West Country; their reputation as fast-running, free-steaming engines won them their nickname. All were withdrawn between 1933 and 1943.

AMERICAN TANKS
See YANKEES.

ANTELOPES
A general purpose MT 4-6-0 introduced on the LNER by Edward Thompson, Gresley's successor. The first emerged from Darlington Works in December 1942, and by 1949 409 more had been added; 340 of them were constructed by NBL and the Vulcan Foundry. Simple and robust 2-cyl locomotives, classified 'B1', they were both popular and hard working, and could be found all over the LNER system. Under BR auspices 14 were loaned to the Southern Region in May 1953 when Bulleid's 'Pacifics' had to be taken temporarily out of service. The first 'B1' was named *Springbok* in honour of General Smuts's visit to the UK, and 40 more were named after other species of antelope, though the name *Antelope* itself was never used. Unofficially they were known as BONGOS, which name, incidentally, was borne by the

ADAMS'S FLYER No 685, seen here at Nine Elms around 1920, spent its last years at Eastleigh, working on local goods and occasional ballasting duties. Withdrawal in February 1936 must have come as something of a merciful release. *Steamchest*

sixth-built of the class. Just before nationalisation 17 more were named after LNER Directors; in 1951 the name *Mayflower* was bestowed upon another, now preserved, as a symbol of Anglo-American friendship. All others remained nameless. Latterly, 17 'B1s' entered Service Stock, and the last two, Dept Nos 30 and 32 (formerly 61050 and 61315) were condemned in April 1968.

ARDSLEY TANKS

A new type of 0-6-0T, introduced by Gresley in 1914. In place of the GNR's long-standing tradition of saddle tanks, the new design incorporated large side tanks which, extending forward to the front of the smokebox, were tapered at the front to assist shunting visibility. Openings were provided in the side tanks to facilitate access to the inside motion. Of 30 locos built between 1914 and 1919, 27 were sent to work in the large marshalling yards around Ardsley, in the West Riding. Gresley added 72 more by 1939, and, again,

many went to Ardsley. Seven, however, were dispatched to Cadder, near Glasgow, where lay the only gravity-worked marshalling yard in the LNER's Scottish Area. By now these strange-looking tanks were a commonplace sight to GNR men. Not so, however, to Scottish locomen who, intrigued by their appearance, promptly christened them CHINESE PUZZLES or SUBMARINES. The tanks were to remain undisturbed at Cadder for 20 years; by 1965, however, all ARDSLEY TANKS, however they were known, or wherever they were located, had vanished.

ARIEL'S GIRDLE

A remarkable little four-wheeled engine, built by Kitson, Thompson & Hewitson of Leeds in 1851, and exhibited as *Ariel's Girdle* at the Great Exhibition in Hyde Park that year. Subsequently purchased by the EUR, the locomotive was employed as No 28 on its Bentley and Hadleigh branch. The original intention was to connect the rear of the

ARDSLEY TANK No 603, built at Doncaster in 1926, and classified 'J50/3', spent most of its life shunting or handling transfer goods. It was withdrawn as BR No 68949 in April 1959. *Steamchest*

engine to a composite carriage, underneath which a tank would be suspended, carrying 533 gallons of water. It was, in other words, an early concept of the steam railmotors which later enjoyed considerable popularity. The loco itself weighed 16 tons. Its own water tank held 304 gallons, and a receptacle over the firebox held 6 cwt of coke. Once *Ariel's Girdle* became ECR No 17 in 1856 its limitations were recognised, and it was converted into a 2-4-0ST at Stratford Works in 1868. Latterly it was sent to work on the Millwall Extension Railway. Ten years later it was replaced by a four-wheeled Kitson steam tram, and was finally broken up in May 1879.

ARMSTRONG GOODS
See STANDARD GOODS.

AUL' BOGIES
When James Manson of the G&SWR renewed the bulk of Stirling's Class '6' 4-4-0s, by then 40 years old, in 1899-1901, the result was another 16 7 ft 1 in engines which were able to work Glasgow–Carlisle expresses in approved Sou' Western style. The new locomotives, known to G&SWR men fondly as the AUL' BOGIES, all graduated to LMSR ownership, but were, alas, only classified '1P'. In keeping with LMS policy towards small classes, the AUL' BOGIES did not last long; the last three were withdrawn in 1930.

AUSTERITIES
This nickname was very much a product of the Second World War, when large numbers of engines designed by R.A. Riddles were built to the order of the Ministry of Supply; all were introduced in 1943. Of the most prolific class, the 2-8-0s, 200 were purchased by the LNER in December 1946, and in 1949 BR took over another 533. Twenty-five AUSTERITY 2-10-0s were also bought by BR in December 1948, and were sent to work mineral traffic in Scotland. A third class of War Department AUSTERITIES, their powerful 0-6-0STs, found havens in many parts of the UK, and many are preserved today. Once

more, the LNER bought 75 from the Ministry of Supply. See also IRON LUNGS.

AUSTRIAN GOODS

A 2-6-0 version of Peter Drummond's (in)famous G&SWR 0-6-0s, the PUMPERS (qv). Eleven were built in 1915, and despite provision of Robinson superheaters and the locos' extra dimensions they still only turned the scales at 4½ tons more than the basic 0-6-0! Some of the material used in their construction by NBL was believed, probably erroneously, to have come from an earlier order which was placed by Austria, but which remained unconsummated because of the outbreak of war. Thus the nickname AUSTRIAN GOODS, or, more colloquially, the BIG AUSTRIANS, attached itself to these engines. Extremely popular with Sou' Western men, the new 2-6-0s replaced the PUMPERS on the 'Long Road Goods', ie Glasgow to Carlisle, and proved themselves very economical locomotives, particularly in the use of water. The last, No 17829, was withdrawn by the LMSR in March 1947.

'B' ENGINES
See STANDARD GOODS.

BABY AUSTINS

These massive-looking 0-8-0s were introduced on the LMSR by Sir Henry Fowler in 1929. Bascially a development of the LNWR 'G2' Class, which, unlike many Crewe-built passenger engines, had not shown themselves inferior under test to current Midland designs, the new 0-8-0s were, nevertheless, very Midland and neat in appearance. In working order, engine and tender weighed nearly 90 tons. One hundred were built in 1929, and 75 more were added by 1932. Despite these large numbers, the performance of this standard LMS locomotive never quite came up to expectations. The locomen's nickname for them, BABY AUSTINS, was, however, as much a reflection of the times in

In this view, LMSR 0-8-0 No 9674, the last-built of 175 BABY AUSTINS, also carried the ACFI feed water heating apparatus which gave rise to a second nickname, HIKERS. *Author's Collection*

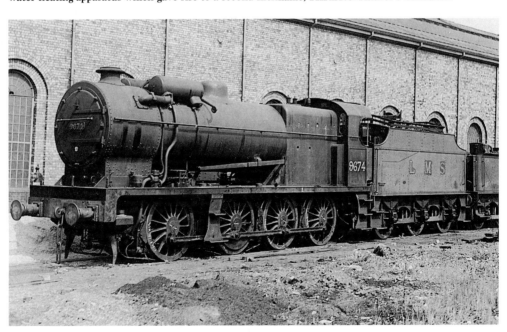

reflection of the times in which they were introduced as anything else. Those which were later fitted with ACFI feed water heating apparatus were additionally known as HIKERS (qv).

BABY SCOTS

Following the introduction by the LMSR of the 'Royal Scot' 4-6-0s in 1927, Crewe Works continued to turn out a number of rebuilt ex-LNWR 'Claughtons' using a large boiler but employing the original 4-cyl chassis. Then, in 1930, Derby Works applied the enlarged 'Claughton' boiler to what was practically a 'Royal Scot' chassis, to create a new LMS 3-cyl Class '5' express locomotive. Two trial engines emerged in 1930. Fowler, CME at that time, intensely disliked the nickname BABY SCOTS which was bestowed upon them, and later they were officially styled 'Patriots'. One shudders to think how Sir Henry might have reacted to yet another nickname by which they were known— WATERCARTS! Patricroft men, meanwhile, chose to dub the new locos CHINESE COMPOUNDS! Ultimately, 52 in all were built. They should, however, be regarded as replacements for, rather than rebuilds of, the original LNWR 'Claughtons'. Efficient and thoroughly reliable machines, most carried names in the long run—an amalgam of ex-'Claughton' names, regiments, and towns which were served by the LMS. Eighteen were rebuilt by H.G.Ivatt during 1946-48 with a large tapered boiler, new cylinders, and double chimney. Reclassified '6P', they were now very similar to W.A.Stanier's earlier rebuild of the 'Royal Scots'.

BALERNOS

Also known as CATHCART CIRCLE TANKS, these 12 0-4-4Ts were introduced on the CR by J.F. McIntosh in 1899; officially they were known as the '104' Class. To meet special suburban requirements, eg close proximity of stations, steep gradients and sharp curves, the diameter of their coupled wheels was reduced to 4 ft 6 in, as opposed to the normal diameter of 5 ft 9 in. Trailing wheels were similarly cut down to 2 ft 6 in. This

improved acceleration when getting away from stations. The little tanks operated successfully for many years on the Balerno (Edinburgh) and Cathcart Circle (Glasgow) circuits, and the last, No 15153, was not withdrawn until April 1938.

BALTICS

See LONG TOM TANKS.

BANTAM HEN

Shortly before his death Gresley designed a special 2-6-2 tender engine to tackle the increasing workloads on the LNER's West Highland route. A small lightweight version of the highly successful 'Green Arrow' type, No 3401 *Bantam Cock*, the first of the class, went straight to Eastfield shed, Glasgow, in 1941. A sister engine, No 3402, which later kept her company, was never named, but Eastfield men soon christened the newcomer BANTAM HEN. Though highly successful in operation, the class proved to be too expensive to justify further reproduction. BANTAM HEN was withdrawn in November 1957, eight months after her companion.

BARNEYS

Nickname given to 12 0-6-0 freight locomotives which were built by Peter Drummond for the HR between 1900 and 1907. Typically Drummond in design, they originally carried safety valves on the dome, and were fitted with firebox water tubes. The latter were removed by the LMSR when rebuilding was effected in 1923-24. All survived the Grouping in 1923, and seven passed into BR ownership. Only three, however, ever carried BR numbers, and the last, No 57695, was scrapped in January 1952.

BARNUMS

A class of 20 double-framed 2-4-0s introduced on the GWR by William Dean in 1889. Their highly ornate and colourful appearance earned them the nickname BARNUMS, after Barnum's Circus, the 'Greatest Show on Earth', which was then appearing in London. Certainly Dean's most famous and successful 2-4-0s, they were probably the

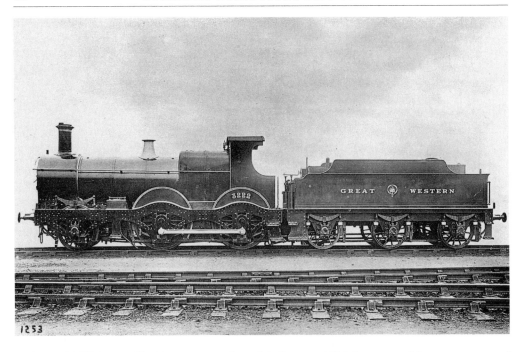

GWR BARNUM 2-4-0 No 3222 was superheated in January 1920, but reverted later to a saturated boiler. The engine was eventually withdrawn from Wellington shed in March 1937. *Author's Collection*

world's last locomotives to be designed with sandwich frames. Most lasted into the 1930s, and all but one achieved one million miles. The last two survivors were withdrawn in March 1937.

BASHERS
These were sturdy double-framed MS&LR 0-6-0s, later LNER Class 'J8'. Really an enlargement of Charles Sacré's earlier goods engines, 12 were built at Gorton Works in 1887-88 to the order of Thomas Parker, Sacré's successor. They were the first MS&LR locomotives to be fitted with a screw reverse. For many years all were stationed at Staveley, where their vigorous employment on both goods and passenger work earned them their nickname. By 1930 all had perished.

BEATTIE'S FOLLY
A disparaging nickname given, probably somewhat unfairly, to the '384' Class express 4-4-0s which were introduced by W.G.Beattie in 1877. Poor Beattie, so much was expected

in 1877. Poor Beattie, so much was expected of him when he succeeded his illustrious father in November 1871! Hard pressed by his Locomotive Committee in 1875 to produce 'larger and more powerful engines', he prepared drawings for a series of large o/c 4-4-0s, weighing 10 tons more than the latest 2-4-0s. Sharp Stewart & Co built 20 for the LSWR, but a combination of sundry mechanical innovations and frequent breakdowns earned the class a bad name.

When the Locomotive Committee called for a full report, Beattie was rash enough to blame bad workmanship on the part of Sharp Stewart. The latter responded by demanding inspection of all 20 locos at Nine Elms, and once this had been accomplished they issued a detailed report declining blame for the failure of the design. Beattie persevered with minor alterations and adjustments, but alas, a final report to the Directors in December 1877, revealing that only four of the class were in regular use, clinched matters; later that month Beattie retired quietly on grounds of ill health. Modern assessment suggests that he was a shade unlucky, and possibly a little ahead of his time in introducing the Class '384s'. These unfortunate locos were also known as JUMBOS.

BEEFEATERS
See SCOTSMEN.

BEETLECRUSHERS
The Class '498' 0-6-0Ts of the CR, and the only o/c design ever created by J.F.McIntosh. Two were built at St Rollox in 1912, and their coupled wheelbase was made as short as possible, at 10 feet, to combat sharp dockyard curves. An extremely compact appearance, plus a working weight of $47\frac{3}{4}$ tons, earned the locos their nickname as they ground their way round the CR's various marine establishments. Twenty-one more were added by W.Pickersgill between 1916 and 1922 to meet increased wartime dockyard demands. The BEETLECRUSHERS were a great

advance on four-coupled saddle tanks previously employed by the CR on dockyard work. All entered BR service, and the last, No 56159, was withdrawn from Polmadie shed, Glasgow, in March 1962.

BELGIANS
A series of 20 5-foot 0-6-0s built by R. & W. Hawthorn & Co for the NER in 1873-74. These engines were nicknamed BELGIANS by NER men because Hawthorn brought in Belgian workers to break a strike at the time they were being built. None survived beyond 1920.

BELLY CRAWLERS
A powerful and versatile class, these 120 superheated 'T2' 0-8-0s were introduced on the NER by Raven in 1913-21. Classified 'Q6' by the LNER, all survived to enter the service of BR. Rarely seen north of Carlisle or Newcastle in their heyday, quite a number, however, worked between Newcastle and

Ex-CR BEETLECRUSHER No 16152, caught off duty at Fouldubs shed in the mid-1930s, was one of a pair which were rebuilt to the order of J.F. McIntosh in January 1912. W. Pickersgill added 21 more over the years 1916-22. *Author's Collection*

Edinburgh in the 1940s. By that time Haymarket and St Margarets men were thoroughly accustomed to handling 'K3s' and 'V2s' on East Coast goods workings, and took not kindly to the older NER locos. Thus in Edinburgh the 'Q6s', with their 4 ft 7¼ in driving wheels, outside cylinders, and absence of leading pony truck, were nicknamed, rather unfairly, BELLY CRAWLERS. All none the less lasted into the 1960s.

BELPAIRES

A nickname which commemorated S.W. Johnson's first use of larger boilers and Belpaire firebox when he produced his '700' Class 4-4-0s for the MR in 1900. Batches followed at regular intervals, and the class totalled 50 by 1904, whence Johnson proceeded to his famous Midland Compound design. Most '700s' were rebuilt with superheaters by Fowler from 1913 onwards, and the last of these was in service until 1953.

Meanwhile, H.S. Wainwright of the SE&CR also perceived a need, in 1905, to anticipate growing express locomotive demands. Thus Ashford Drawing Office, by incorporating a Belpaire firebox in an expanded 'D' Class design, was responsible for the construction of 26 new 'E' Class i/c 4-4-0s over the years 1905-09. Soon known to SE&CR men as BELPAIRES, the new engines put in intensive mileages during the First World War. Eleven were rebuilt with, amongst other things, larger Belpaire fireboxes in 1920. Ironically, Class 'E' became extinct in May 1955, more than a year before the last (older) Class 'D' was withdrawn.

BELPAIRE GOODS

A final class of 0-6-0 goods engine, introduced by the Cambrian Railways in 1903, and the first Cambrian engines to be built with a Belpaire firebox. Five were supplied by R. Stephenson & Co in 1903, while Beyer Peacock followed with four more in 1908, plus a final five in 1918-19. Good strong engines, all passed into GWR ownership at the Grouping. Three were withdrawn in 1922, but the remainder lasted into the 1950s.

BEYERS

Such was the sound reputation of Beyer Peacock & Co for building locomotives that Daniel Gooch of the GWR was content in 1864 to order 20 0-6-0 engines, and leave the design entirely to the company. Two years later, 10 more were ordered by Joseph Armstrong. They were most efficient and handsome locos, with gracefully curved double frames and open brass-rimmed splashers. Later some were rebuilt as tank engines. During their hard-working careers most of the BEYERS accumulated healthy mileages. No 354, one of three which registered 1½ million miles, was the last survivor before bowing the knee in August 1934.

BICYCLES

A group of six engines, the first 2-4-0s to be built at Swindon, brought out in 1868. Unusually ugly for GWR locos, they had platforms of broad gauge style which curved over the driving wheels to form rim splashers, hence their nickname. The locos' appearance was considerably improved when all six were renewed at Wolverhampton in 1885-86. Each of the one-time BICYCLES achieved well over one million miles, and put in nearly 50 years' service before being withdrawn during the First World War.

BIG AGGIES
See RODs.

BIG AUSTRIANS
See AUSTRIAN GOODS.

BIG BENS
See WEE BENS.

BIG BERTHA

This nickname was first given to a huge gun which was employed by the Germans during the First World War, the reference being to the Krupp heiress. Over a period of years, meanwhile, the MR was considering fresh solutions to the problem of banking trains up and over the Lickey Incline. Finally, in 1919 Derby Works built a massive 0-10-0, the second of that wheel formation to be pro-

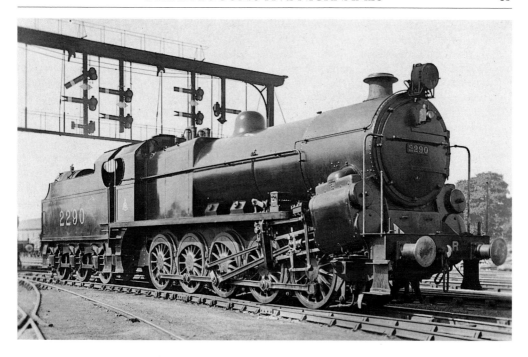

BIG BERTHA, the MR's powerful banking engine, stands by at Bromsgrove, complete with headlight, shortly before the Grouping. Renumbered 22290 by the LMSR in August 1947, it was withdrawn as BR No 58100 in May 1956. *Steamchest*

duced in Great Britain. Naturally this new monster created something of a sensation— and BIG BERTHA she became. Some referred to her as BIG EMMA, a phonetic variation on 'M for Midland'. All four cylinders drove on to the centre pair of 4 ft 7½ in wheels. The loco herself weighed 73½ tons, and her specially-built tender cab added 31½ tons. Thus the total working weight was 105 tons. A duplicate of her huge superheated boiler was kept at Derby Works for periodic refitting. The 0-10-0 soon justified her nickname, for her assistance from the rear on the bank proved equal to that of a brace of the MR's most up-to-date 0-6-0Ts. Though most of BIG BERTHA's life was spent working up and down the 2-mile stretch of the Lickey Incline, the loco still managed to put in a mileage of 838,856 before retiring in 1956. A power headlight, fitted in 1921 and run by a turbo-generator on the footplate, was duly handed on to her successor, BR 2-10-0 No 92079. See also DECAPOD.

BIG BOGIES
Even swifter than the WEE BOGIES (see GREENOCK BOGIES) were Hugh Smellie's G&SWR BIG BOGIES of 1886-89. Kilmarnock shopped 20 of these 6 ft 9½ in 4-4-0s; some were fitted with removable extended smokeboxes, and all had domeless boilers, though some were later domed. Whatever, Sou' West men, with their love of hard running, worshipped the BIG BOGIES. No 65 was scrapped after a collision in February 1898, but the remainder lived to pass into LMSR stock. The last to be withdrawn, No 14143, went in November 1935.

BIG EMMA
See BIG BERTHA.

BIG GOBBLERS
Dugald Drummond was determined to produce a successful large 4-6-0 for the LSWR. While some doubt exists as to whether or not he succeeded, there can be no doubt that

doubt that many of the eccentricities he built into his larger locomotives were a grievous trial to those who worked beneath him. His first 4-6-0s emerged from Nine Elms in 1905, and other designs followed at regular intervals. Perhaps those that were most unkind to locomen were his five Class 'P14' of 1910-11, by now products of Eastleigh Works. Though they were superior to their immediate predecessors, the 'G14s', in handling West of England expresses, the 'P14s' exercised an insatiable appetite for coal. The consequent human toil and sweat which accompanied any routine schedule they undertook soon, therefore, earned them the heartfelt sobriquet of BIG GOBBLERS. All except one were scrapped by R.E.L. Maunsell, the SR's new CME, in January 1925. The survivor, No 449, was only spared awhile to act as a mobile test bed for Maunsell's proposed new 'Lord Nelson' Class 4-6-0s; it eventually followed its sisters in October 1927.

BIG SWAMIES
See SWAMIES.

BILL BAILEYS
The LNWR's first eight-coupled freight engine was built by F.W.Webb in 1892, and formed the prelude to a long line of similar locomotives, most of which passed into LMSR hands in 1923. Webb was totally preoccupied with the problem of compounding, and when his Class 'B' 4-cyl compound 0-8-0s, and similar mixed traffic 4-6-0s, began to emerge in 1901 their inevitable eccentricities earned them the cheerful nickname of BILL BAILEYS, after the popular music hall song of 1903. It was perhaps a blessing that LNWR locomen met Webb's maniacal perseverance in the matter of compound locomotives with such good humour. The nickname of JOHNNY DUGANS was also used. See also PIANO FRONTS.

BISSEL TANKS
See BOX TANKS.

BLACK ALICE
See GALLOPING ALICE.

BILL BAILEY No 2024 looks conventional enough in this portrait, but these four-cylinder compound 0-8-0s gave the LNWR many a hilarious moment. *Steamchest*

BLACK BESS

This 0-6-0ST, built by Fox Walker & Co (Maker's No 338) in 1877 as one of a pair for the Great Yarmouth & Stalham Light Railway, bore when shopped the name *Stalham*. After passing through sundry minor East Anglian railway ownerships, it was eventually admitted to M&GNJC stock in 1893, still bearing Eastern & Midlands Railway number 16. Duplicate listed as 16A in 1905, the saddle tank spent the remainder of its M&GNR/LNER life as Works shunter at Melton Constable, where it was affectionately known as BLACK BESS. When the Works was closed by the LNER in 1937, BLACK BESS was condemned on 25 October of that year, and was cut up at Stratford.

BLACK BILLY

Surely this is one of the oldest locomotive nicknames, bestowed upon the first engine delivered to William Hedley at Wylam Colliery in 1813. Built by Thomas Walters of Gateshead, the locomotive was a Trevithick type, with one 6-inch cylinder and a flywheel, but no return flue. Hedley built a second engine himself, a much more successful machine, with two vertical cylinders driving an arrangement of beams. Known locally as PUFFING BILLY, it was sent to South Kensington Museum in 1865, and can still be seen there as 'the oldest locomotive in existence'.

BLACK FIVES

One of many successful W.A. Stanier designs for the LMSR, and certainly his most prolific. A straightforward 2-cyl MT 4-6-0, found latterly in every region of BR, the first in service was No 5030, built by the Vulcan Foundry in September 1934; eventually the class consisted of 842 engines, of which Crewe built 241, Horwich 120, Derby 54, Armstrong Whitworth 327, and Vulcan Foundry 100. The original locomotives, numbered in the 5000 series and painted black, soon became popularly known as the BLACK FIVES. Quite a number were experimentally modified in a variety of ways, eg different types of valve gear, roller bearings, double chimneys, steel firebox, etc. Officially the class became

BLACK BESS was carrying M&GNR number 16A when it was photographed at Melton Constable Works shortly before the establishment was closed down by the LNER in 1937. *Author's Collection*

extinct in 1968, but more than 20 have been preserved in various parts of the country. On the Highland Section of the LMS, the Class '5s' were also known as HIKERS (qv) because of their ability and willingness to stride along, whatever the load. The BLACK FIVES were also frequently referred to as BLACK STANIERS.

BLACK MOTORS

These sturdy 0-6-0s were introduced on the LSWR by Dugald Drummond in 1897. Dubs & Co supplied 30 at a cost of £2,695 apiece, their design based largely on a similar type Drummond had already provided for the CR in Scotland. Despite their official designation as Class '700', the nickname BLACK MOTORS followed these LSWR engines all through life; it is difficult to imagine why, for in LSWR days they were painted dark green. Extremely versatile engines, the BLACK MOTORS were adept at handling special trains and excursions, as well as fast goods. After the First World War most were modernised and fitted with superheaters, and the SR completed the process after the Grouping. All survived to pass to BR, and more than half of them saw in 1962 before they were scrapped.

BLACK PIGS

Also known to GCR men as COLLIER'S FRIENDS, J.G. Robinson's last and most numerous 4-6-0 type, Class '90', were massive-looking black machines, possessed of an inordinate appetite for coal. Four-cylindered, and designed for MT work, 28 were built at Gorton during 1921-22, while the LNER added 10 more in the immediate post-Grouping years. Restyled Class 'B7', the class remained intact until 1948, whence subsequent withdrawals saw all vanish by February 1950. Despite locomen's harping on their hunger for coal, the BLACK PIGS had a good turn of speed and were useful for fast goods and passenger relief work: many an excursion sailed forth behind a 'B7'. As they were really a small-wheeled version of the earlier 'Lord Faringdon' ('B3') express 4-6-0s, the BLACK PIGS were also known as the FARINGDON GOODS.

BLACK STANIERS
See BLACK FIVES.

BLACK TANKS

Four massive Class 'G16' 4-8-0Ts, designed by Robert Urie for the LSWR in 1921 to handle hump shunting duties at Feltham marshalling yard. They were given a black livery by the SR, hence their nickname. Conversely, the 'H16' 4-6-2Ts, built for kindred purposes, were painted green (see GREEN TANKS). All 'G16s' were withdrawn by December 1962.

BLACKWALL TANKS

In 1889 J.Holden produced 10 0-6-0 passenger tanks, designed for light duties on the GER; 10 more were added in 1893. The class, later 'J65' under LNER auspices, had early associations with Fenchurch Street–Blackwall traffic, and thoroughly succeeded in stabilising the 15-minute morning to evening service which was operated thereon. Soon known as the BLACKWALL TANKS, the little locos ran frequently as 2-4-0Ts, with the front portion of the siderods removed. Withdrawal of the Blackwall services after the General Strike of 1926 saw the 'J65s' move to East Anglia. Scrapping commenced in 1930, but four lived to pass into BR hands, and the last, No 68214, was not withdrawn until October 1956.

BLOCK TANKS
See FLAT IRONS.

THE BLOOMER

Nickname given to a 5-foot 2-4-0 which was supplied by Beyer Peacock & Co to the G&SWR in 1858. Similar in design to the LSWR's 'Medusa' Class, the Scottish loco entered G&SWR stock as No 109 *Galloway*, though, for some reason, the name was soon removed. Handsome and popular though the locomotive was, it was replaced in 1874. The nickname BLOOMER was no doubt inspired by the divided firebox it carried.

BLOOMERS

Bloomer costume was introduced in America

by Mrs Bloomer of New York in 1849. When she visited the UK the fashion was adopted by a few in the West End of London in about 1851, but was later discarded under ridicule. None the less, the comparative immodesty of the dress was enough to attach the nickname to engines then emerging which showed more of the wheels than was customary. The most celebrated BLOOMERS were the LNWR 2-2-2s of 1854-61, designed by J.E. McConnell. Appropriately they came in sizes. The SMALL BLOOMERS had 6 ft 6 in driving wheels, but lacked adhesion, and by 1876 all were relegated to minor duties. LARGE BLOOMERS had 7-foot driving wheels, and it is said that Crewe did not deploy this class to its best advantage. Whatever, all BLOOMERS had inside frames and axle bearings, and no cabs.

BLUEBOTTLE
A 2-4-0T built by G. England & Co for show

at the International Exhibition of 1862. Purchased by the Somerset Central Railway in October 1863, the little well tank was beautifully painted in deep blue, and this may well have inspired the blue livery which was adopted by the S&DJR in 1886. The 2-4-0WT, numbered 11, was sold to the Admiralty, at Sheerness, in 1886. See also DAZZLERS.

BONGOS
See ANTELOPES.

BOXERS
The first UK locomotives to feature horizontal outside cylinders, these were 2-2-0s designed by George Forrester of Liverpool in 1834, three for the Dublin & Kingstown Railway, and a further pair for English use. The combination of o/c and short wheelbase guaranteed, in the event, much swaying and uncomfortable motion at speed, and the

LARGE BLOOMER. Built at Wolverton Works in April 1862, and intended to be LNWR Southern Division No 395, this 7-foot 2-2-2 was absorbed instead into a unified LNWR stock as No 995. Ten years later it was given the name *Briareus*, and withdrawal came only too soon, in 1879. *Author's Collection*

engines were soon dubbed BOXERS. Their design, however, led to later development of the 2-4-0 type. The three Irish locomotives were soon converted to tanks, and were further unique in possessing *three* sets of frames. See also TAILWAGGERS for a GNR version of the BOXERS.

BOX TANKS
A series of 20 LNWR 0-4-2Ts, built in 1896-1901 with square pannier tanks. They were designed by F.W. Webb for dock work and employment on branches with sharp curves—thus 4 ft 5½ in driving wheels were employed. All passed into LMSR ownership, but though withdrawals commenced in 1929 the last, BR No 47862, was not scrapped until November 1956. In light of their solid trailing wheels, these engines were also known as BISSEL TANKS.

BRASSBACKS
During his career with the LB&SCR Robert Billinton fitted a number of his 'B2' and 'B4' 4-4-0s with direct-loaded safety valves in brass columns. These were mounted either fore and aft or transversly over the firebox, and their distinctive shape soon earned them the nickname 'bathing drawers'. The engines themselves acquired the nickname BRASS-BACKS. See also GRASSHOPPERS.

BRICK ENGINES
See LONG TOMS.

BROAD STREET RATTLERS
For a comparatively modestly-sized concern, the NLR ran an extremely intensive suburban passenger service. During the year 1898, for instance, 71 NLR trains worked in and out of Broad Street station during the 9-10 am 'rush hour'. A small 4-4-0T type, initiated by William Adams in 1863, and further developed by J.C. Park, his successor in office, monopolised NLR suburban traffic, and, seen careering along at the head of long

BOX TANK No 47 was shopped by Crewe Works in 1899. Seen here in the mid-1920s, as LMS No 6407, it was renumbered 7857 in November 1927, and was withdrawn exactly two years later. *Author's Collection*

The first LB&SCR tender engines to have leading bogies, these Class 'B2' 4-4-0s were known variously as B BOGIES, GRASSHOPPERS and BRASSBACKS. No 319 was built at Brighton in 1896 as *John Fowler*. Renamed *Leconfield* 10 years later, it retained that name until SR green livery was applied in July 1924. Withdrawal came in April 1930, with a cumulative mileage of 1,187,621. *Author's Collection*

trains of close-coupled four-wheeled coaches, they soon became affectionately known as the BROAD STREET RATTLERS, or, simply, RATTLERS. Four of Adams's i/c tanks survived the Grouping, but never carried LMS numbers. All 74 of Park's o/c type entered LMSR stock. Many never bore their allotted numbers, and of those which did the last went on to 1929. Numbered 6445, it was retained at Derby Works with preservation in mind, but unfortunately was broken up in 1932.

THE BRUISER

A Northern Irish 'odd man out' with a self-explanatory nickname. No 5 in Ballymena & Larne Railway (narrow-gauge) stock was a 2-6-0ST, built by Beyer Peacock (Works No 1947) in 1880. The B&LR's most powerful locomotive, it offered locomen a punishing ride, but was dearly loved for its ability to handle heavy coal and freight trains in and around Larne. After becoming No 109 in B&NCR stock the saddle tank soldiered on as before, and finished up with a total of 900,000 miles before bowing the knee in 1934.

BRUTES

See WEST END TANKS.

BUCK JUMPERS/BUCKS

In tackling suburban traffic generated at Liverpool Street station the GER made great use of 0-6-0Ts, and 261 engines of various classes of this hard-working type were handed over to the LNER at the close of 1922. Thereafter nearly 100 tanks of the 'J69' Class continued as of yore to work the intensive suburban 'Jazz' services to and from Enfield Town and Chingford. By now Ilford and Romford had also been developed as residential areas, and

The famous BUCK JUMPERS were obviously a source of pride to GER men. No 168 was one of 10 Class 'R24' 0-6-0Ts which were built in 1901, complete with condensing gear, for passenger duties on the GER's busy London suburban complex. Later LNER Class 'J69', it was withdrawn as No 7168 in 1940. *H. Gordon Tidey/Lens of Sutton*

tial areas, and the 'Jazz' settled down to a regular interval service of 24 trains per hour. The term 'Jazz' was inspired by the fact that 1st and 2nd class compartments of these busy trains were identified by coloured stripes. The 'J69s' carried on until 1925, when larger tanks became available. Meanwhile, the fore and aft motion they generated at speeds above 40 mph earned them the nickname BUCK JUMPERS, or, simply, BUCKS. With driving wheels only 4 feet in diameter, the tendency was, perhaps, forgivable. One 'J69', withdrawn in 1960 as BR No 68633, was restored to full GER regalia at Stratford Works, and is now part of the National Collection at York.

After the Grouping 'J69s' wandered widely on the LNER system, and 20 found their way to Scotland in 1927-28. At St Margarets shed, viewed with some circumspection, they were labelled COFFEE POTS. In Fife, on the other hand, where they were employed on yard and dock shunting duties, they were

known as TAR TANKS. Probably their stove pipe chimneys and squashed-looking appearance evoked recollections of the tar boilers used in road surfacing. See also JUBILEE JUMPERS.

BUFFALOS

William Dean of the GWR believed in making extensive use of 0-6-0STs, and was responsible for building a large number for branch-line passenger and freight work, and even long-distance goods trains where circumstances allowed. His '1076' Class, 266 of which were built between 1870 and 1881, was the last of the double-framed variety, and their rugged appearance, plus hauling power and tenacity, earned them their nickname. Later they followed GWR current practice by being converted into the more familiar square pannier tanks. Particularly tough engines, withdrawals commenced in 1903, but the last of the BUFFALOS soldiered on until 1946.

THE BUG

Dugald Drummond, the LSWR's Locomotive Superintendent, liked to travel around to see for himself how his Company's affairs were progressing, and for this purpose he had a private locomotive built at Nine Elms, with a small saloon attached behind the cab. Costing £1,765 to build, this odd little 4-2-4T entered service in June 1899. Known officially as 'Mr Drummond's Car', it earned a rather less respectful reputation amongst LSWR men as THE BUG. Drummond also used it to travel daily from his home at Surbiton to Nine Elms, and later to Eastleigh. To LSWR men the sight of THE BUG approaching was no light matter, for Drummond was a martinet, albeit a fair one, who did not tolerate fools gladly. Up to the date of his untimely demise in 1921 his remarkable little machine ran a total of 361,804 miles.

Drummond's successor, Robert Urie, was also a Scot, but he had little use for the machine, either temperamentally or physically. Thus the duties of 'Mr Drummond's Car' lapsed into little other than occasional inspection tours. The latter were conducted in such a different atmosphere, however, that the one-time BUG now became known as THE PET OF THE LINE. Later, in 1932, the SR's Publicity Department shrewdly employed the little machine to conduct important visitors round Southampton Docks. In August 1940 a final decision was made to dismantle the engine; but even then the frames of THE BUG continued to haunt Eastleigh Works for a good few years to come.

BULLDOGS

The first BULLDOGS were a group of five unusual 0-4-0Ts built for the SER by R. Stephenson & Co in 1851. They embodied an odd arrangement whereby an intermediate, or 'dummy', shaft replaced what might have been a third, and central, pair of driving wheels. At first these engines were sent to Folkestone, to handle steep curving work on

This LB&SCR BULLDOG, 'D' tank No 239 *Patcham*, was built by Neilson & Co (Works No 2708) in November 1881. It was one of only a handful which saw in 1948, and the little tank was withdrawn as SR No 2239 in March of that year. *Steamchest*

the Harbour branch. They suffered badly from lack of adhesion, however, and at times it was found that all five had to be employed in tandem to handle a single train. Cudworth decided to rebuild them as conventional locomotives, and all five returned to Folkestone in the late 1850s as 0-6-0Ts. Mansell 0-6-0Ts took over in 1877, whence withdrawal of the BULLDOGS was rapidly effected.

The 1870s were also a period of rapid expansion where LB&SCR suburban services were concerned. Stroudley's TERRIERS (qv) had already proved a brave success on South London Line traffic, but new tanks, with greater speed and enhanced coal and water capacity, were needed to cope with increasing outer suburban demands. Thus, in 1874 Stroudley's immortal 'D' tanks emerged. So useful did they prove to be in all types of work that the little 0-4-2Ts also acquired the nickname BULLDOGS—despite their modest dimensions. In all, 125 were built, and most enjoyed an equally active life under SR auspices; remarkably, the last, No 2284, formerly

Ashburnham, by then No 701S in Service Stock, was not withdrawn until December 1951.

A third class of BULLDOG emerged when Charles Sacré built his largest 0-6-0s for the MS&LR. Sixty-two of these sturdy engines were shopped from Gorton Works in 1880-85, and their nickname was inspired by the ruggedness of their substantial double frames. Popular with enginemen, they found plenty of heavy goods work to tackle in the South Yorkshire area. In 1921, due to arrears of maintenance work at Gorton, 12 GCR BULLDOGS travelled to Erith, Kent, for overhaul at Vickers works. After the Grouping, however, the re-introduction of large numbers of ex-ROD 2-8-0s to LNER stock saw to their replacement, and during the 1920s the number of BULLDOGS diminished rapidly. The last, LNER No 6428, was withdrawn in February 1930. Interestingly, once Robinson began fitting BULLDOGS with Belpaire fireboxes in 1909 the species looked even tougher.

Amongst several others the S&DJR, too, had its BULLDOGS. One of 10 0-6-0s supplied between 1896 and 1902, No 43216, seen here at Cole in 1958, was the last to be withdrawn, in August 1962. *Author*

Another class of BULLDOGS, though born in England, acquired their nickname through Scottish connotation. Nigel Gresley's powerful-looking Class 'N2' 0-6-2Ts first appeared on GNR suburban metals in December 1920. Condensing apparatus and a short Metropolitan-gauge chimney gave the 'N2' such a puissant appearance that it still seems surprising that nicknames were not applied to the class until 20 of them, with reduced boiler mountings, were sent to Scotland seven years later. By early 1929 44 'N2s' were operating north of the Border, but though they were thoroughly competent engines NBR men were never happy with them. Those built after the Grouping featured left-hand drive, and this helped, but by and large the 'N2s' were considered crude and uncomfortable by Scottish crews. Fitters at Cowlairs did not care for them either, and the big tanks were also heavy on the permanent way. Thus, the various nicknames by which the 'N2s' were known in Scotland tell their own tale. The term METROPOLITANS bespoke a certain irreverence for anything which came from London; the sobriquet BULLDOGS implied both power and brashness. The kindest 'N2' nickname came from the Scottish railway enthusiasts who, relishing the rather snug appearance of the 0-6-2Ts, dubbed them TEDDY BEARS.

Even the S&DJR had its BULLDOGS. These were a group of 10 0-6-0s, half of them built at Derby Works, half of them supplied by Neilson & Co, in 1896 and 1902 respectively. Nine survived to enter BR stock, and the last, No 43216, was not withdrawn until August 1962.

Undoubtedly the most famous BULLDOGS of all were William Dean's celebrated outside-framed GWR 4-4-0s. This class, however, acquired its title by association with a locomotive name, and thus falls outside the ambit of this book.

BUS PUGS

These were 10 0-4-4Ts, built by Neilson & Co for the G&SWR in 1893, and designed by James Manson to handle Glasgow suburban work. These local services were traditionally known as 'Bus Trains', and, as on every Scottish railway, a tank engine was known as a PUG; thus the little tanks became known as the BUS PUGS. All survived to pass into LMSR stock, and the last pair were not withdrawn until 1932.

BUSTERS

These were Class 'B4' 4-4-0s, 32 in number, which were introduced on the LB&SCR by R.J. Billinton in 1901-02. The first 20 were to have been built at Brighton, but after three had been completed it was found that heavy repair commitments made further progress impossible. Sharp Stewart & Co, when approached urgently on the matter, supplied 25 at a cost of £3,990 each. Later five more were added at Brighton. Because of their bold proportions, compared to those of previous LB&SCR 4-4-0s, the 'B4s' soon became known as BUSTERS. Inevitably, as most were constructed in Glasgow, the nickname SCOTCHMEN also attached itself to the class. The locomotives were extremely popular with Brighton men, and although withdrawals commenced in 1934, a dozen which were rebuilt as Class 'B4X' hung on until 1951. So, too, did four unrebuilt BUSTERS. See also GREYBACKS.

BUTTERFLIES

The first locomotives of this ilk were 18 2-4-0s which were designed for GER goods and passenger traffic by J.V. Gooch. Six each were built by Canada Works, Sharp Stewart, and Kitson & Co in 1855-56, and it was probably the dainty appearance of the little locomotives which gave rise to the nickname BUTTERFLIES. Alas, like their namesakes, life was comparatively short, and all perished by 1879.

Another aspect of butterfly life was exemplified in 1897, when Dugald Drummond introduced his first large express locomotive for the L&SWR. Following F.W. Webb's 'divided drive' example, Drummond opted to employ four high-pressure cylinders to drive two pairs of uncoupled driving wheels. In the event, results with Drummond's solitary Class 'T7' 4-4-0 No 720 were no better than

Webb's. Wheelslip proved to be a major problem, and it was established latterly that the two inside cylinders were, in fact, performing 68 per cent of the work. Undaunted as ever, Drummond built five more 'double singles' in 1901, classified 'E10'. These were marginally better, but, despite the fact that all six locomotives lived to enter SR stock at the Grouping, finding constructive use for them proved to be an almost impossible task. Thus all went to the wall by 1927. Their nickname was a reflection on their unreliability, and the frequent shop visits they required: according to LSWR men, the BUTTERFLIES were liable to appear on fine summer days, when traffic was at its height—then disappear for the rest of the year!

THE CAB

This nickname was given by NBR men to one of a pair of Neilson-built 1850 vintage 2-2-0WTs, originally supplied to the Caledonian & Dumbartonshire Junction Railway, and absorbed by the Edinburgh & Glasgow Railway in 1862. Built to Adams patent as a combined locomotive and coach, it was rebuilt in 2-2-2T form in 1858, and latterly engine and coach were separated. It entered NBR stock in 1865 and, when it was again rebuilt in 1868, a quite substantial saloon, or cab, was added. So useful did the little loco prove to be as an inspection saloon that it was rebuilt yet again in 1882 and 1895. It served the NBR well until 1911, when it was sold. Dugald Drummond's admiration for THE CAB no doubt inspired his construction of THE BUG (qv) on the LSWR in 1899.

CALEYS

In November 1939 the War Department, having adopted W.A. Stanier's LMSR 2-8-0 as its standard goods engine, had large numbers of these locomotives built by both private contractors and main-line railway

workshops. In view of their unequivocal LMS design those which wandered into the LNER Scottish Area during the years 1945-47 were inevitably dubbed CALEYS by former NBR men. Indeed, to the latter, steeped as they were in Scottish railway history, anything connected, however remotely, with the LMSR generally attracted the CALEY (Caledonian) label!

THE CAMEL

No 68 *Mark Lane*, built by NBL (Works No 15749) in 1903, was one of the LT&SR's famous TILBURY UNIVERSAL MACHINES (qv). Later renumbered MR 2175 and LMSR 2109, this engine ran for a while with a top feed injector. The sight of what appeared to be two domes in close proximity was enough to earn No 2109 the nickname THE CAMEL. Though allocated BR No 41926, the locomotive still carried its LMS number when it was withdrawn in March 1951.

CAMELS

To LMS men, well used to the graphic lines of the Horwich 2-6-0s (see CRABS), the appearance of W.A. Stanier's new MT 2-6-0 came as something of a shock when the first 15 entered traffic in 1933. The tapered boiler, and the dome flanked by the top feed pipes—even with a safety valve in some instances—persuaded some LMS men to hail the new arrivals as CAMELS. See also LOBSTERS.

CANAL No 1

A Barclay 0-4-0ST (Works No 12) purchased by Monkland Navigation in 1862. It was Monkland's only engine, hence the nickname. The locomotive was not taken into stock when the CR purchased the canal concern in 1867. Presumably, however, the little saddle tank worked on elsewhere, for it was not scrapped until 1889.

CARRIE NATION

On one occasion, after discontinuance of rope haulage on Cowlairs Incline in 1908 by the NBR, the 1.5 pm express from Edinburgh got out of control when descending the bank

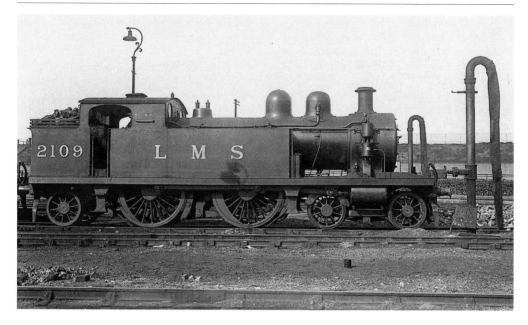

The LT&SR's **TILBURY UNIVERSAL MACHINE** No 68 *Mark Lane,* later LMS No 2109, was dubbed **THE CAMEL** over the period it ran with a top feed injector. This Shoeburyness shed photograph explains why. *S.J. Rhodes*

and dashed into a crowded Glasgow (Queen Street) station on a Saturday afternoon. No one was seriously hurt, but the runaway engine made such a thorough job of demolishing the station bar that many NBR men thereafter referred to No 595 as CARRIE NATION, the name of a well-known contemporary US temperance reformer.

CATHCART CIRCLE TANKS
See BALERNOS.

CATRINE CAUR
During the railmotor craze at the turn of the century, James Manson of the G&SWR entered the lists by having three 0-4-0WT railmotors constructed at Kilmarnock Works in 1904-05. Only No 3 had engine and coach separated, the idea being to avoid excessive vibration. All three were used in turn on the Catrine branch, which opened on 1 September 1903, but closed again during the First World War. Whichever incumbent was operating on the branch, it was invariably referred to as the CATRINE CAUR. The branch

eventually re-opened after the cessation of hostilities, but the CATRINE CAURS never returned; all three were scrapped in 1922.

CAULIFLOWERS
These versatile and hardy 0-6-0s were mass-produced for the LNWR by the indefatigable F.W. Webb; 310 were built between the years 1880 and 1902, weighing 36½ tons and emplying Joy's valve gear. Very smart locomotives in general appearance, the ornate LNWR crest they carried on the central splasher inspired some gardening wag one day to dub the locomotives CAULIFLOWERS; and so they remained for ever more. Even with 5 ft 2½ in driving wheels, the CAULIFLOWERS had a fair turn of speed, and were often used on passenger trains. In January 1937, for instance, a speed of 74 mph was recorded when No 8369 handled a 280-ton train between Penrith and Carlisle. First scrappings took place in 1918, but no fewer than 69 of these tough little engines survived to meet nationalisation in 1948. They were also known as CRESTED GOODS.

In similar amused context, LB&SCR monograms, as applied in very ornate fashion to locos at the turn of the century, were known irreverently as RASPBERRIES.

CHANCELLORS
See ENGLANDS.

CHARLIES
See UTILITIES.

CHINESE COMPOUNDS
See BABY SCOTS.

CHINESE CRACKERS
When six 0-6-4Ts, destined to handle heavy coal trains, were ordered by the LD&ECR from Kitson & Co in 1903, the makers allowed themselves some latitude in design. The resultant mixture of Belpaire firebox, GNR-type chimney and a very unsightly forward extension to the smokebox was enough to earn these engines the nickname CHINESE CRACKERS. Three more, delivered in 1905, reverted to more conventional appearance. Despite their massive-looking potential, however, the 0-6-4Ts' duties were taken over by 0-6-0 and 0-8-0 tender engines once the GCR took charge. The CHINESE CRACKERS finished their days largely on shunting duties; the last, by then 'M1' Class No 9082, was withdrawn by the LNER in July 1947.

CHINESE FOURS
A BR Doncaster-designed development of H.G. Ivatt's LMSR 'Mogul' of 1947 (see FLYING PIGS). With greater coal capacity and a very low axle loading of under 17 tons, the BR Standard '3MT' Class, 115 in number, was introduced in December 1952, and proved to be extremely popular in the Southern and Scottish Regions. The combination of '4MT' power classification, route availability 4, and their somewhat bizarre appearance earned these locos their nickname, particularly in the Scottish Region. At least four have been resuscitated, and now work on preserved lines in the UK.

CHINESE PUZZLES
See ARDSLEY TANKS.

CHIPCARTS
These tiny NBR 0-4-0STs, later LNER Class 'Y9', were found around Leith Docks and sundry sidings for many years, and in the Falkirk area at least they were known as CHIPCARTS. This arose from the dipping and weaving motion they generated when travelling light, reminding onlookers of the horse-drawn carts which once dispensed fish and chips around the town. Actually the 'Y9s' were a tough little breed. Built between 1882 and 1899 at Cowlairs Works, all 35 entered LNER stock in 1923, and only one fell by the wayside ere BR took over in 1948. No 68095, the last to go in December 1962, was secured for preservation by Lytham Power Museum. They are generally presumed to be Holmes engines, but the first two were in fact ordered by Dugald Drummond from Neilson & Co in 1882, and were of that firm's standard design.

CHIP VANS
A nickname, in similarly sardonic vein, bestowed on the LNER's green and cream 100 hp Sentinel railcars, built in 1928-29, which served in the Scottish Region. These cars were never very popular with firemen, many of whom referred to them as SWEAT BOXES.

CHITTAPRATT
A vertical-cylindered 0-2-2-0 which was built by Robert Wilson & Co of Newcastle, and was taken into Stockton & Darlington Railway stock as No 5 *Stockton*. It was not a success, however, and the locomotive was withdrawn after meeting with an accident at Stockton in October 1826. The boiler was salvaged, none the less, and was later used for *Royal George*. The nickname CHITTAPRATT is generally believed to have been inspired by the loco's unusual exhaust sound.

CHOO-CHOOS
See STUPID Ds.

Ex-NBR CHIPCART No 9040 rests on its laurels at Dunfermline shed. Built at Cowlairs in 1897 as No 40, it survived a fall into the water at Kirkcaldy harbour, and, classified 'Y9' by the LNER, it was the last ex-NBR 0-4-0ST to remain in Fife. Note the class plate 'G' on the cabside, and the shunter's steps fitted below. Both were hallmarks of NBR practice. *Steamchest*

CHOPPERS

Whatever his demerits, F.W. Webb served the LNWR extremely well when it came to turning out large quantities of simple hardworking engines. In 1879, for instance, Crewe Works built No 71, the first of a long line of 4 ft 6 in 2-4-2Ts whose construction went on to 1898. These tough little tanks would tackle anything, from station pilot duties to main-line services, and their sharp exhaust, plus the inflexible motion of their coupling rods at speed, earned them both respect and the nickname CHOPPERS. Ninety-three of them were passed on to the LMSR in 1923, but all perished within a decade. An alternative school of thought maintains that the nickname CHOPPERS applied only to five of these tanks, when they were cut down to 2-4-0T from in 1905, and were motor-fitted. See also MOTOR TANKS.

LES CHURCHILLS

See DEAN GOODS.

CLAN GOODS

A series of eight o/c 4-6-0s designed by Christopher Cumming in 1917 to tackle goods traffic on the severely graded HR main line. Built by Hawthorn Leslie with 5 ft 3 in coupled wheels, they coped admirably. Two years later, Cumming, by adding 6-foot wheels, developed the design into his justly famed passenger 4-6-0s, the 'Clans'. Again built by Hawthorn Leslie, it is of interest to note that individual locomotive costs had risen by now from £4,920 to £6,957. In the event, the express 4-6-0s gave yeoman service, and because they were named after Scottish Clans it was only a matter of time before their freight equivalents of 1917 acquired the nickname CLAN GOODS. Five of the latter survived to carry BR run-

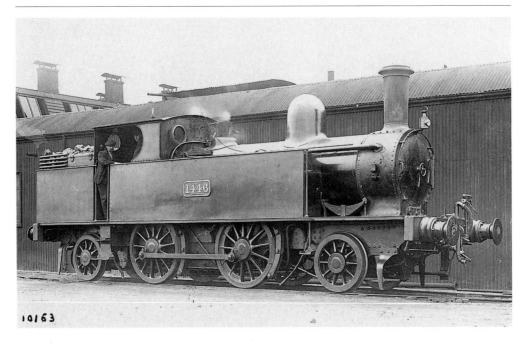

10163

One of a long line of CHOPPERS, LNWR 2-4-2T No 1446 (Works No 2844) emerged from Crewe Works in 1885. Nearly 40 years later, it was allotted LMS No 6562, but was withdrawn in March 1926, still carrying LNWR identification. *Author's Collection*

ning numbers, and the last, No 57954, was withdrawn in October 1952. All the passenger 'Clans' had gone by then.

CLANKERS
See RAGTIMERS.

CLATTERBANGS
A development by M. Kirtley of his 'M' Class 4-4-0s for the LC&DR. Known as Class 'M3', 26 were built, mostly at Longhedge Works, between 1891 and 1901; the last three went straight into SE&CR stock. Speedy locomotives, they handled boat trains during the early 1900s, after which Wainwright's Class 'Ds' took over. Even then, four 'M3s' were kept in first class condition during the First World War, to work 'Imperial Special BS' trains which ran, often at very short notice, between Victoria and Dover Harbour, conveying VIPs, dispatches and couriers to and from the Western Front. The 'M3s' ran freely and fast, and were liked by men who were experienced in their ways. Mechanically they

were very noisy, and it was this idiosyncrasy which earned them their nickname. All entered SR stock in 1923, but as increasing numbers of 'King Arthurs' and 'L1s' became available the need for CLATTERBANG services diminished. Thus all had vanished by September 1928.

CLAUDS/ CLAUD HAMMIES
CLAUDS was the generic name for J. Holden's impressive new 4-4-0s, the pride of the GER in 1900; they were also known as CLAUD HAMMIES. The prototype emerged from Stratford Works on St Patrick's Day, and, in addition to being specially numbered 1900, it was given the name *Claud Hamilton*, after the Company's Chairman. Promptly displayed at the 1900 Paris Exhibition, the locomotive's sheer elegance gained her a Gold Medal. Various annual batches then followed from Stratford, until 111 locos of the class existed by 1911. Unusually, they were numbered in reverse, from 1900 to 1790. Superheating was introduced with No

The last three CLATTERBANGS, the LC&DR's popular Class 'M3' 4-4-0s, entered service in 1901 carrying SE&CR numbers. No 464, however, left Longhedge Works in March 1897 bearing LC&DR No 5. Stationed at Faversham when the Grouping was effected, it met early retirement, as SR No A464, in April 1926. *H. Gordon Tidey/Lens of Sutton*

1793, and No 1803 was rebuilt with a larger boiler and other refinements, and was shopped from Stratford in March 1923 as the first SUPER CLAUD. A few months later 10 last CLAUDS were turned out from the same Works.

Powerful and delightful engines, it was no surprise that a CLAUD was responsible for the longest non-stop run ever made by a GER locomotive, when, in June 1907, No 1848 hauled a Press Special from Liverpool Street to Sheringham (142½ miles) in 2 hrs 58 mins. The same engine hauled Queen Alexandra's funeral train from Kings Lynn to King's Cross on 26 November 1925, this time in LNER livery. The LNER, in fact, took a very active interest in developing the type, which ultimately acquired seven different classifications, ranging from 'D14' to 'D16/3'. In all, 117 CLAUDS survived to pass into BR

stock, and the last, No 62859, was not withdrawn until May 1959. They were very dear to GER men's hearts.

CLODHOPPERS.
See FLYING PIGS.

CLYDE BOGIES
This rather contradictory nickname for HR locomotives arose simply from the fact that they were built by the Clyde Locomotive Works. This company was formed when Walter Neilson left Neilson & Co, and the Clyde's first engines, in 1886, were eight 4-4-0s of a David Jones design. The last delivered, No 76 *Bruce*, gave its name to the class, and the loco was shown at the Edinburgh Exhibition of that year. Although the CLYDE BOGIES were soon to be superceded by further Jones 4-4-0 classes, they hung on

The Clyde Locomotive Works built only 30 engines during its brief independent career, and half of these were for South American Railways. Its first order, however, for eight 4-4-0s, came from the HR, and all were completed in 1886. CLYDE BOGIE No 76 *Bruce*, the last of the eight, was proudly exhibited in Edinburgh that year, and served the HR until 1923. *Author's Collection*

almost to the Grouping. One apparent survivor, LMSR No 14277, even worked on into the 1930s. It transpired later, however, that this engine did not belong to the 'Bruce' Class, but was an erroneously numbered SKYE BOGIE (qv).

COAL ENGINES

Yet another of F.W. Webbs's prolific classes for the LNWR, 500 of these simple 0-6-0s were built at Crewe between 1873 and 1892. One, No 1140, was built and steamed in a record working time of 25½ hours, although this record was later shattered by the GER, when 0-6-0 No 930 was erected and steamed at Stratford Works on 11 December 1891 in a world record time of 9¾ hours (see STONES).

Weighing only 32 tons, the LNWR COAL ENGINES were considered by E.L. Ahrons to be 'probably the simplest and cheapest locomotives ever built'. The first to be withdrawn went in about 1903, the year in which

Webb retired, but 227 of these tough little engines survived to assume LMSR numbers in 1923, and 46 of them were still in service at nationalisation. The last, BR No 58332, was withdrawn in October 1953.

In the early part of 1874, one year after the first of Webb's COAL ENGINES emerged from Crewe Works, the GWR had 20 of the small-wheeled version of its STANDARD GOODS (qv) built at Swindon. Numbered 927-946, most of them spent their working lives at Birkenhead, where they handled coal trains to and from Pontypool Road. Known consequently to GWR men as COAL ENGINES, their lifetime mileages varied between three-quarters to one million miles. The last survivor, still based on Birkenhead, was withdrawn in August 1925.

COAL GOODS

These were sturdy little 0-6-2Ts designed by F.W. Webb for LNWR coal traffic. With driving wheels of only 4 ft 3 in diameter, 300

Hundreds of these sturdy **LNWR COAL ENGINES** were turned out from Crewe Works between 1873 and 1892, and many of the class led chequered careers before retiring from service. The life of No 433 (Works No 1638), one of the 1873 batch, was, however, rather prematurely terminated when the locomotive was cut up in 1906. *Author's Collection*

were built at Crewe between 1881 and 1896. Only nine had gone by the Grouping, but though 64 survived nationalisation all vanished within 10 years. The ultimate survivor, BR No 58926, built in 1888, has been preserved in original LNWR livery as No 1054, and, owned by the National Trust, is presently on loan to Dinting Railway Centre. See also CRYSTAL SETS.

COAST BOGIES
See GOUROCK BOGIES.

COFFEE POT
The very first engine constructed by the SER in its Ashford shops was nicknamed COFFEE POT. A four-wheeled tank, it was a curious vertical-boilered affair. Construction commenced in September 1850 and the total cost was £438 10s 8d. After a somewhat undistinguished career the little tank finished up as a stationary engine at Redhill, before being sold in 1888 to a Newhaven scrap merchant

for the princely sum of £26 18s 10d.

Also known as the COFFEE POT, because of its vertical boiler, was an 0-4-0T which was supplied by T.H.Head to the Dorking Greystone Lime Co Ltd in 1871. Its frame of cast iron was made in one casting, wheels were of 2 ft 4 in diameter, and cylinders were 6 in x 12 in. The locomotive was probably built by Head Wrightson & Co Ltd of Thornaby.

Meanwhile, eight flat-topped o/c 0-4-0STs were constructed for the GER between 1874 and 1903, the first four by Neilson & Co, with Stratford Works adding the remainder in 1897 and 1903. They were odd little locos. One of them, LNER No 7230, survived as Stratford Carriage Works shunter until 1948. Maintained in fully-lined black livery, it shone like a button and appeared frequently, styled the COFFEE POT, at LNER exhibitions which were staged throughout the 1930s. Eventually this delightful little engine, LNER Class 'Y5', was withdrawn in 1948.

An early COFFEE POT, this vertical-boilered locomotive, probably an 1871 product of Head Wright-son of Thornaby, served the Dorking Greystone Lime Co for many years. *Steamchest*

The next COFFEE POTS were not far removed from GER influence, for they belonged to the Millwall Dock Co. The latter's goods and passenger responsibilities extended little over 1½ miles, between Millwall Junction and the Docks—yet by 1872 a full passenger service was in operation, with GER locomotives taking over from Millwall Dock horses at the southern boundary of the Docks! The MDC next purchased three small Manning Wardle 2-4-0Ts, and a full steam service, using hired GER coaches, started on 23 August 1880. The tall chimneys and spark arresters of the Manning Wardles soon earned them the nickname COFFEE POTS. Rebuilt in 1905, the three COFFEE POTS came under Port of London Authority aegis in 1909, and carried on as of yore until November 1922.

During the year 1924 10 ex-NER Class 'J24' 0-6-0s were transferred to the LNER's Scottish Area, to be used on light branch work on place of aging Wheatley and Drummond ex-NBR types. In Scotland the 'J24s' were not highly regarded, despite their usefully powerful steam brake; at St Margarets shed, Edinburgh, probably because of their brass safety valve covers, they were referred to as often as not as COFFEE POTS. None the less, the last 'J24' to go, BR No 65617, ended its days at St Margarets in December 1951. See also BUCK JUMPERS.

COLLIER'S FRIENDS
See BLACK PIGS.

COLTS
When J.G. Robinson succeeded H. Pollitt as GCR Locomotive Engineer in June 1900 his first express locomotive design was a series of 40 Class '11' i/c 4-4-0s. Anticipating later Robinson 'Atlantics' and 4-6-0s, they took over the working of the GCR's London Extension from Pollitt's 4-4-0s, and fared

very well when Sam Fay speeded up GCR services in 1905, their nimbleness and general utility earning them the nickname COLTS. No 1014, named *Sir Alexander* in 1902 after the Company Chairman, was the first MS&LR/GCR engine to bear a name since 1859, when Charles Sacré had all names removed. Three other COLTS were named after members of the Royal Family, and, as LNER Class 'D9', all 40, ever popular in Cheshire, served also in many other areas, including East Anglia. The last, No 62305, was withdrawn in July 1950.

COMBINE HARVESTERS

A not inappropriate nickname given to BR's last Standard steam design, the massive 2-10-0s of 1954. With 5-foot driving wheels and a tractive effort of just under 40,000 lbs, these formidable machines could handle anything from passenger excursion traffic to the heaviest mineral trains. Several have been preserved, including No 92220 *Evening Star*,

the last built, which was turned out from Swindon in March 1960. See also SPACE SHIPS.

COMPOUNDS

Although F.W. Webb and sundry other locomotive engineers wrestled vigorously with the problems of compounding, the 19th century closed without conspicuous evidence of success. The more remarkable it is, therefore, that the MR, devoid of experience in the matter, was able to produce in 1902 a 4-4-0 compound design which was eventually to form the basis of a class of 250 locomotives. Well might MR and LNWR men be forgiven for annexing the term COMPOUND as their own!

The first two MR COMPOUNDS, designed by S.W. Johnson, were shopped from Derby Works in January 1902, and R.M. Deeley, Johnson's successor, followed up with 10 of his own version in 1905. Thirty more were built by 1909. All passed to the LMSR in

Both LMSR products of 1925, COMPOUND No 1126 and CR-type GREYBACK (qv) No 14630 head a Glasgow–Aberdeen express through Larbert in July 1935. In the event, No 1126, withdrawn in October 1956, outlived the 4-6-0 by just over five years. *Author*

due course, and history relates how that august concern saw fit to add 195 more of these remarkable locomotives to its stock; 190 alone were built in 3½ years. Nor did the MR COMPOUND fail them, for, driven by men who understood their potentialities, they were superb locomotives. Men in the Scottish Region were particularly drawn to their combative qualities, and only the introduction of large numbers of Stanier 4-6-0s dislodged the COMPOUNDS from exclusive express work. After a spell of secondary duties, January 1953 saw the last of the Midland COMPOUNDS, though the prototype, No 1000, was retained to take her rightful place in the National Railway Museum at York. The LMSR COMPOUNDS just outlived the construction of BR's last steam locomotives, and the last was not withdrawn until 1961. Whether in MR or LMSR crimson lake livery, a COMPOUND at its best was always a handsome sight, and no one could grudge an alternative nickname, the CRIMSON RAMBLERS, by which they were known. See also RED DEVILS.

CONCRETE MIXERS

An uncomplimentary nickname bestowed upon LNER Class 'L1' 2-6-4Ts, 100 of which were introduced by Edward Thompson in 1945-50. In practice they seemed to develop an unpleasant corkscrew motion when running at speed, probably due to poor balancing of the class with its long tanks. Later, in the mid-1950s, LNER men working empty stock trains in and out of King's Cross station had occasion to confirm the nickname CONCRETE MIXERS—this time because of the noise the 'L1s' created!

CONNEL BUS

This was the popular nickname for a converted motor charabanc which had been used earlier by the CR to provide a road service from Clarkston station to the village of Eaglesham, in Renfrewshire. Probably a 30 hp

Although the prototype CONCRETE MIXER was built at Doncaster in 1945, the remaining 99 engines of this LNER 'L1' 2-6-4T class were shopped between January 1948 and September 1950. No 67742 was a NBL product (Works No 26581) of November 1948, and was one of the last batch to be withdrawn, in December 1962. *Author's Collection*

Thorneycroft, rebuilt for the purpose at St Rollox Works, the vehicle was then used, somtimes hauling two carriage trucks, to ferry passenger across the Connel Bridge to North Connel, where connection was made with the CR's Ballachulish branch. The service, which began in June 1909, was rendered redundant in 1913, when a roadway was added to the railway line on Connel Bridge.

CONVERTED 30s

The CR's Class '30' was a group of powerful 0-6-0s which was built at St Rollox to the order of J.F. McIntosh in 1912. That same year McIntosh, by lengthening the frame of his design, introduced five i/c 2-6-0s. Weighing 54¼ tons, and later classified '3F' by the LMSR, the 'Moguls' were, not unnaturally, referred to by CR men as CONVERTED 30s. The last-built, LMS No 17804, was withdrawn as the sole survivor in May 1937.

CONVERTED TANKS

When Barton Wright introduced 280 sturdy

0-6-0 tender engines in 1876-87 to L&YR stock, no one but his successor, J.A.F. Aspinall, could possibly have visualised that 230 of the class would be converted into equally sturdy 0-6-0 saddle tanks 15 years later. All the STs duly entered LMSR stock, and 101 even survived to function under BR auspices. Five of the class, employed as works shunters at Horwich, retained their LMS numbers for some time in BR service, and one of these, latterly numbered 51305, was last to go, in 1964. See also IRONCLADS.

CONVERTIBLES

As a result of the 'Battle of the Gauges', broad gauge tracks had almost disappeared from the GWR system by 1875. Only a certain untidiness in the West Country remained, and to meet a shortage of locomotives in that area Joseph Armstrong fitted 10 standard gauge 0-6-0STs, then under construction at Swindon, with broad gauge axles; the wheels were placed outside the frames. These were known as CONVERTIBLES. William Dean on his

No 16, a GWR CONVERTIBLE 2-4-0 designed by William Dean, was one of a pair which were built at Swindon in June 1888, specifically to work the heavy 3 pm up express from Bristol to Swindon. Having served their West of England purpose, the two erstwhile broad gauge engines were renewed as standard gauge 4-4-0s in 1894. *Steamchest*

accession in 1877 continued the policy by supplying various other types. Once the Broad Gauge era ended in May 1892, all remaining CONVERTIBLES were quickly altered for standard gauge use.

COPPERNOB

FR 0-4-0 No 3, known as COPPERNOB because of her bright domed copper firebox, was a superb example of early Bury locomotive construction. Built in 1846 at a time when the Stephensons, father and son, were still active, COPPERNOB was one of Bury, Curtis & Kennedy's famous bar-framed tender engines. After an industrious career with the FR right up to 1900, the little engine was displayed for many years in a glass case outside Barrow-in-Furness station. Fortunate to escape severe damage after an enemy air raid during the Second World War, the locomotive was later lodged in Clapham Railway Museum. It is now, of course, a prime exhibit at the National Railway Museum, York.

COPPERTOPS

After H.S. Wainwright of the SE&CR had spent some time considering the relative merits of Horwich and Doncaster-built 'Atlantics' and the CR's famous 'Dunalastair' 4-4-0, he designed his 'D' Class 4-4-0s. Ashford Works contributed 21 between 1901 and 1907, and outside firms provided another 30. No 735, built by Sharp Stewart & Co, was proudly exhibited at the Glasgow Exhibition of 1901. Beautifully liveried in green, with much polished brasswork and a copper-capped chimney, the Class 'Ds' subsequently captured the public imagination, and were known by one and all as COPPERTOPS. No 1726 was condemned after an accident in 1947; otherwise all passed to BR. One of the last survivors, withdrawn in November 1956, is now preserved, restored to former SE&CR glory, in the National Railway Museum, York. This locomotive achieved a lifetime mileage of 1,694,660.

COPPERTOPS were well appreciated in pre-First World War years, and the SE&CR's 'D' Class 4-4-0 No 488, built at Ashford in 1902, shows how H.S. Wainwright's gleaming Brunswick green livery was enhanced by boiler mountings of burnished brass. It cost all of £41.68 to paint a Class 'D' in 1910! *Steamchest*

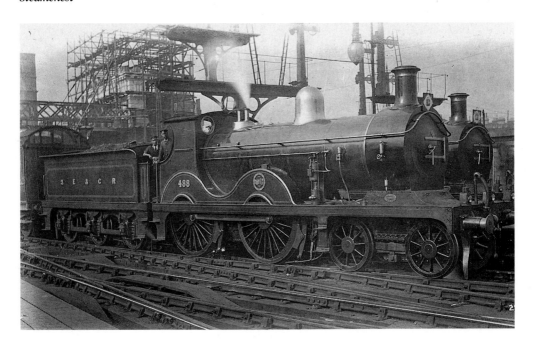

Further north, the NER was also well known for the elaborate finish of its passenger locomotives. Twenty Class 'M1' i/c 4-4-0s, introduced by Wilson Worsdell in 1892-94, looked particularly handsome with their 7 ft 1¼ in driving wheels. So too, did 30 Class 'Qs' which were added in 1896-97. The two classes later became 'D17/1' and '17/2' in LNER stock. Then, when 'Atlantics' displaced the Class 'Qs' from East Coast Main Line services from 1910 onwards, many of the 4-4-0s were allocated to provincial sheds. London Road, the NER's shed at Carlisle, eventually received 12, for use on the Carlisle–Newcastle service. Very proud of their new charges, NER men christened them COPPERTOPS, and kept them in immaculate condition. The last of the Carlisle contingent, No 1926, was condemned in 1931, only two years before the shed was closed. Fortunately, No 1621, the second-built of the 'M1' Class, was retained for preservation when it was withdrawn in July 1945. It can now be seen in all its elegant NER green livery at the National Railway Museum, York.

CORKY LIZ
When W.A. Stanier produced his two massive 'Princess Royal' 'Pacifics' in 1933 the GWR pedigree embodied in their construction was readily apparent. One such modest detail, the provision of corked oil boxes, designed to keep dirt out without occasioning an air-lock, so impressed some LMS drivers that they nicknamed No 6201 *Princess Elizabeth* CORKY LIZ!

CORONATION TANKS
King George V was crowned at Westminster Abbey on 22 June 1911. That same year a new class of i/c 4-6-2T, J.G. Robinson's last passenger tank design, was introduced on the GCR, and nothing seemed more natural than that these handsome new engines should attract the nicknames CORONATION and ABBEY TANKS. Twenty-one were built at Gorton between 1911 and 1917 and, testament to their worth, 23 more were added by the LNER in 1923-36. Built primarily for

lengthy suburban workings in and out of Marylebone station, the big tanks performed admirably. So, too, did a further 13 which were constructed by the LNER in 1925-26 for use in the North Eastern Area. Of the 1911 'originals', No 5447 was scrapped in 1942, but 15 more years elapsed ere the next was withdrawn; the very last trio, Gorton-built to a man, did not bow the knee to diesel railcars until November 1960. Regrettably, none has been preserved.

COUNTY TANKS
In 1904 G.J. Churchward introduced his most unsuccessful class, 30 o/c 4-4-0s, named after English and Irish counties. These were followed in 1905 by a tank version, this time of 4-4-2 wheel arangement. The intention was to employ the new tanks on short-distance passenger work, and in view of the similarity of design they soon became known as the COUNTY TANKS. Outside cylinders and four-coupled wheels did not, however, cohabit happily on either class, and much uncomfortable travel resulted. By 1925 both the 'Counties' and the COUNTY TANKS had disappeared.

CRAB AND WINKLE
This affectionate nickname was bestowed upon GER Class 'S44' 0-4-4T No 1121 when the loco worked the Brightlingsea branch in pre-Grouping days, and the nickname was passed on to subsequent sister engines which worked the branch. Forty of these tanks were built at Stratford in 1898-1901, all passed into LNER stock as Class 'G4', and the last of J. Holden's nippy little locos survived until December 1938.

CRABS
In 1914-17, when J.G. Robinson reversed the wheel arrangement of his handsome 'Pacific' tanks to produce 20 new i/c 2-6-4Ts, the results were so disappointing, aesthetically speaking, that GCR men nicknamed them CRABS. Intended primarily for coal traffic in the Midlands, the locos' brake power, however, proved to be incommensurate with their haulage capacity, and most were

Even a shapely Robinson chimney could not conceal the ungainliness of the GCR's Class 'L1' CRAB 2-6-4Ts. No 9061, seen here as LNER Class 'L3', was one of 18 which were added by Gorton Works in 1915-17. It lasted until February 1953. *Steamchest*

switched to local goods traffic around the Chesterfield area. Despite fluctuating careers, and the basic shortcomings of the class, they lasted remarkably well; classified 'L3' by the LNER, all but one passed into BR ownership. No 69069, the last-built as it happened, was not withdrawn until July 1955. The first-built, No 5292 (later 69050), acquired a nickname of its own, the ZEPPELIN, when it went to Retford to pursue lonely shunting duties. This nickname was also applied to two more of the class which served at Frodingham.

Also known as CRABS were the LMS standard o/c 2-6-0 MT locomotives first seen in 1926. The remarkable appearance of these engines, with cylinders set high, and at a sharp angle to their raised footplate, easily earned them their nickname. Oddly, the origin of these CRABS was Scottish, for at the Grouping the CR had a similar machine almost ready for production. Alas, its large horizontal cylinders would have fouled most UK loading gauges. G. Hughes, the LMSR's CME, was, however, impressed by the design,

and, using the same power characteristics, developed therefrom his famous CRABS. By the time construction had commenced Sir Henry Fowler has succeeded Hughes; nevertheless, though Fowler added a few Midland features such as a tender narrower than the cab, the basic Horwich design was faithfully retained. In all 245 were built, in almost equal proportions, by Crewe and Horwich Works between 1926 and 1932. Successful and efficient, they were soon to be found all over the LMSR system, working freight or passenger as required. Many went north of the Border, where they lent ready aid to rather hard-pressed CR and HR areas. Five were provided with Lentz valve gear in 1931; 21 years later the same engines were rebuilt with Reidinger valve gear, but no significant advantage seems to have been gained by the experiment. Fortunately, the class prototype, No 13000 (later BR No 42765), has been preserved by the Keighley & Worth Valley Railway.

In some areas the LMSR's ubiquitous 'Moguls' were known as FROTHBLOWERS.

CRESTED GOODS
See CAULIFLOWERS.

CRIMSON RAMBLERS
See COMPOUNDS.

THE CROCODILE
The first 4-6-0 on the GWR, and one of the earliest examples of the type in the UK, No 36, William Dean's powerful goods engine, was shopped from Swindon in August 1896. Its wide firebox was probably the first borne by a main-line engine in Britain, and both driving wheels and swing-link bogies were inside-framed. Though it never wandered far from Swindon during its lifetime, No 36 proved itself capable of handling Severn Tunnel line goods trains much more expeditiously than the double-headed freight locomotives normally employed. Thanks to its length and quite startling appearance, the new 4-6-0 was soon nicknamed THE CROCODILE. The only one of its class, however, its was withdrawn in December 1905, and was scrapped with a modest mileage of 171,428.

CROSS LEGS
A group of three 2-4-0s which were built in 1847 by R. Stephenson & Co for the York & Newcastle Railway. The nickname came from the odd motion arrangement the locomotive sported.

CROYDON ENGINES
LB&SCR 2-4-0s Nos 1 and 2, built at Brighton Works in 1854, were intended for work between London and Croydon, and were consequently always referred to as the CROYDON ENGINES. Built at a cost of £2,430 each, they were neat little engines, with inside bearings to the coupled wheels and outside for the small leading wheels. Both were rebuilt in 1863, and No 2, the last to go, was withdrawn in May 1880.

CRYSTAL PALACES
These were the smallest of several classes of

Seen when it was working at Galashiels in the early 1930s, No 8301, one of the GER's delightful CRYSTAL PALACE 2-4-2Ts, offers a clear view of its capacious cab. Popular with Scottish locomen, these tanks were also known as TOMATO HOUSES. *Steamchest*

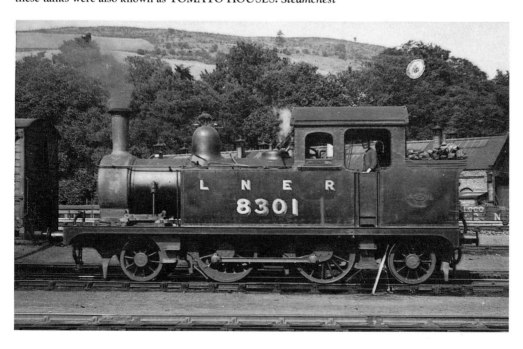

GER 2-4-2Ts, and were designed by S.D. Holden. Bulit in 1909-10, they were later classified 'F7' by the LNER. The chimneys of these delightful little engines had brass rims, and their very large cabs, with windows to the side, front and rear, earned them their nickname. Only 12 were built, and originally they were used for light branch work; latterly they performed on 'auto' push-pull trains around London. The last pair were withdrawn in November 1948. A handful which were sent to Scotland in September 1931 were soon dubbed TOMATO HOUSES by men at St Margarets shed, Edinburgh.

CRYSTAL SETS
Another popular simple type by F.W. Webb for the LNWR was his 0-6-2T, of which 300 were built in 1881-96 (see also COAL GOODS); 80 'Radial' tanks, with larger 5-foot driving wheels, followed in 1898-1902. Both types were hard-working and popular, and seem, regardless of class, to have been known as CRYSTAL SETS or GADGETS. Two 'Radials' survived to enter BR stock, but only lasted to 1953. The COAL TANKS were a side-tank version of Webb's earlier 0-6-0 COAL ENGINES (qv), and were quite often used on passenger work as well. The 'Radials', a tank version of the CAULIFLOWERS (qv), were designed primarily for suburban passenger work.

D

DALKEITH COAL ENGINES
During its first phase of life the NBR built up an initial stock of 71 engines between the years 1846-52. All except one came from R.&W. Hawthorn of Newcastle. Six double-framed 0-6-0s, Nos 27-32, emerged from Hawthorn's shops in 1846, and as they were destined to handle Lothians coal traffic they soon became known as the DALKEITH COAL ENGINES. Three were later rebuilt, and the remaining trio, Nos 29, 31 and 32,

were sold in 1855. In the interesting convolutions which followed, No 29 eventually became NLR No 29 before being sold on to oblivion in 1861, and No 32 was sold to the Marquis of Londonderry's Railway, where it assumed No 4. It was rebuilt as a saddle tank in 1875. The three remaining NBR stalwarts remained in service until 1886-93.

DARTFORD BOGIES
See MAIDSTONES.

DAZZLERS
The S&DJR acquired four delightful 0-4-0STs during the years 1882-95 whose mission in life was to shunt coal traffic at Radstock. The first, built by Slaughter Gruning & Co in 1852, was bought second-hand in 1882, while the other three were built at the S&DJR's Highbridge Works. Apart from being liveried in S&DJR Prussian blue, the STs were so smartly maintained by their crews that they became a local legend and were known as the DAZZLERS. The last entered LMSR stock as No 1509 in 1930, and dazzled on until December of that year.

DEAN GOODS
Successors to Armstrong's STANDARD GOODS (qv), 260 DEAN GOODS were built at Swindon in 1883-89, this time with inside frames. In May 1917, 62 of these wide-ranging locomotives went to France on war service. Again in 1939, 100 were called up for duties abroad; French people often referred to the DEANS as LES CHURCHILLS. After Dunkirk some were used on French railways by the German occupation forces. Others were destroyed by enemy action, and after the war 25 found their way to China in the form of UNRRA relief. Extreme simplicity and utter reliability made the Dean 0-6-0s popular wherever they went, and quite a number lasted well into the 1950s. No 2516 is preserved today in the GWR Museum at Swindon.

A particularly interesting chapter in the lives of 20 DEAN GOODS was their rebuilding in 1907 as Churchward i/c 2-6-2Ts, to meet increased passenger traffic demands in the Birmingham area.

DECAPOD

Ironically, when James Holden of the GER built Britain's first ten-coupled locomotive in 1902, at a cost of £5, 000, his aim was diversionary rather than revolutionary. Two Bills were about to be presented to Parliament sponsoring construction of electrified railways from the City of London to its northeastern suburbs. These presented a serious threat to the GER's suburban traffic, and Holden, taking up the challenge on steam's behalf, decided to demonstrate that a steam locomotive could match electric propulsion by accelerating a train from a dead start to 30 mph in 30 seconds.

The result was a startling 80-ton 3-cyl 0-10-0 well tank, turned out from Stratford Works in December 1902. On test the locomotive did, in fact, accomplish Holden's aim, on a train of 18 suburban coaches weighing 335 tons, although it soon became obvious that track and bridges would not long stand up to the stresses of No 20's frequent passage. Fortunately for the GER, however, the giant loco's prowess helped to stave off the two Bills, and the 'Jazz' continued unhindered. Left with little else to do, the DECAPOD, as she was known, was rebuilt in 1906 as an o/c 0-8-0 tender engine, still bearing running number 20. Posted to March, she showed little improvement over the 0-6-0s in current use there, and the engine was finally cut up in 1913. See also BIG BERTHA.

DEERSFOOT

As completion of the Royal Border Bridge, Berwick, approached, the NBR decided to acquire two high-speed 'prestige' engines. One, costing £2,800, was a Crampton-type 2-2-2-0, built by E.B. Wilson & Co of Leeds Foundry, and was given number 55. Driving wheels were 7 feet in diameter. The other, No 57, also a 7 footer, was built by Hawthorn. A 2-2-0, it cost £ 2,375, and was later named *The Queen*. There is no direct evidence to show how the Crampton behaved on the road, but NBR drivers nicknamed No 55 DEERSFOOT, and regarded it as 'the fastest

James Holden's extraordinary GER DECAPOD 0-10-0 well tank only lasted four years in this form, and was eventually cut up, as 0-8-0 No 20, in 1913. *Steamchest*

engine on the NBR'. Both engines were operating by June 1849. No 55 was rebuilt many times, and was not withdrawn until May 1907, by which time it had acquired a Drummond boiler and Holmes cab.

DIRECTORS

Disappointed by the poor performance of his six 'Sir Sam Fay' 4-6-0s, J.G. Robinson hastened back to his GCR drawing-board and almost immediately scored a resounding success by designing his 6 ft 9 in Class '11E' i/c 4-4-0s. All 10 engines, built in 1913, were named after members of the GCR Board, and were always henceforth referred to as DIRECTORS. They quickly established themselves as Robinson's most outstanding design to date, and were responsible for several remarkably speedy runs on main-line service. Classified 'D10' by the LNER, all survived into the early 1950s. A later version, the IMPROVED DIRECTORS, 11 engines built at Gorton in 1919-22 and classified '11F', proved even more popular. All found employment at Neasden, and only in the late 1930s did six-coupled engines replace them on the GCR main line. Most of them, reclassified 'D11' by the LNER, lasted to 1960, and No 62660 *Butler-Henderson* remains with us as part of the National Railway Collection.

At the Grouping the NBR Section of the LNER badly required reinforcements in the way of express passenger locomotives, and Gresley, reluctant to hasten a new design of his own, selected the IMPROVED DIRECTORS as an admirable choice. Work was given to outside contractors, Kitson and Armstrong Whitworth, and in 1924 24 SCOTTISH DIRECTORS, fitted with lower chimneys, flattened domes, and lower cab roofs to conform with the NBR loading gauge, made their debut in Scotland. By July 1926 all were named after characters from Sir Walter Scott's writings. Notwithstanding initial vexation at having to switch to right-hand drive, and some impatience at the DIRECTORS' inability to get off the mark smartly, ex-NBR men soon developed enormous respect for their new charges. The arrival of 'D49' 4-4-0s in 1928-29, and the subsequent impact of the Class 'B1' 4-6-0s from 1946 onwards, undermined the SCOTTISH DIRECTORS' near monopoly on NBR express traffic. Eventually withdrawals commenced in September 1958; many spent long periods in store, and the last was not withdrawn until November 1961.

THE DIVER

The recipient of this particularly unfortunate nickname was No 224, the Wheatley NBR 4-4-0 which, with five carriages, plunged 80 feet into the River Tay when the Tay Bridge collapsed on 28 December 1879. Built in 1871 as one of a pair, and, indeed, the UK's pioneer i/c 4-4-0, No 224 was subsequently raised from the river bed, repaired, and restored to service. Six years later Matthew Holmes rebuilt her experimentally as a 4-cyl compound, but in 1887 the engine was restored to simple expansion. Nevertheless, to the end of her days she remained known to NBR men as THE DIVER. Withdrawal finally came in 1919.

DOCK PUGS

These were neat little 0-6-0STs, with 3 ft 8 in wheels, designed for the CR by Dugald Drummond; six were shopped from St Rollox Works in 1888. Their duties lay in dockland, and in view of Scottish practice anent tank engines (see PUGS) they readily became known as the DOCK PUGS. Four of them never carried LMSR numbers, and the last was scrapped in 1929.

DOCK TANKS

A more modern LMS version of the same theme, these dainty o/c 0-6-0Ts were introduced in 1928 to supplement existing dock shunting requirements. Designed by Sir Henry Fowler, 10 were built at Derby and were originally numbered 11270-9. Their 9 ft 6 in wheelbase and working weight of 43½ tons served them well in short-radius curve work on many British docks; Fleetwood, Liverpool, Glasgow, and Leith all found use for their services. All continued under BR colours until diesel propulsion gained its monopoly in the 1960s.

NBR men never forgot Wheatley 4-4-0 No 224's involvement in the Tay Bridge disaster of 1879, and the nickname THE DIVER dogged the locomotive until her dying days in 1919. *Author's Collection*

This Works photograph of the prototype LMS DOCK TANK, No 11270, underlines the compact nature of the 10 0-6-0Ts which were designed by Sir Henry Fowler in 1928. Twice renumbered, the class was eventually withdrawn, bearing Nos 7160-69, in 1959-63. *Author's Collection*

DOG'S HOME SHUNTERS
See STEAMROLLERS.

DOLLY GRAY
See HUMPTY DUMPTIES.

DONKEYS
See NAGS.

DOODLEBUGS
A nickname used by GWR men when referring to AUSTERITY (qv) 2-8-0s as the latter infiltrated GWR territory during and after the Second World War. The locomotives were functional enough; but, of course, their spare, uncompromising appearance clashed somewhat with customary GWR aesthetics! See also FLYING PIGS.

DOUBLE BREASTERS
Like Webb on the LNWR, Dugald Drummond in his LSWR days nursed a passion for experimentation. Many a locomotive eccentricity he produced was bravely borne by those who served under him, but possibly his most startling contribution was the five massive 6 ft 7 in 4-6-0s he had built in 1911, classified 'T14'. With all four cylinders located directly under the smokebox, the large casing which was required to join these two elements gave the engines an almost grotesque appearance; when viewed from the front, the significance of their nickname, DOUBLE BREASTERS, was easily understood. An alternative name for these monsters, PADDLEBOXES, was earned by the huge splashers Drummond conjured up to accommodate the coupled wheels and outside valve gear. Though far from a total success, the 'T14s' at least acquitted themselves better than Drummond's earlier 4-6-0s. But bad steaming was still a problem, and unless handled by men who understood their ways, the 'T14s' made heavy going of express work. Drummond added five more in 1912, and Urie later added superheaters to all 10 of the class.

Urie's successor, R.E.L. Maunsell, rebuilt

Known to LSWR men as DOUBLE BREASTERS and PADDLEBOXES, Dugald Drummond's four-cylinder 'T14' 4-6-0s were as formidable as they looked. All 10 were rebuilt by Maunsell in 1930-31, and No 443 lasted until May 1949. *Author's Collection*

the lot in 1930-31 with a raised running-plate and much smaller splashers, the aim being to facilitate cooling of the axle boxes. Many were stored by 1939, then the outbreak of war offered them a new lease of life. Subsequently, a variety of duties came their way—until November 1948, when three of the nine which remained were taken out of service. Regular withdrawals followed, and the last DOUBLE BREASTER, No 461, went in June 1951 with a total mileage of 1,054,620. No 458 had the doubtful distinction of being mortally damaged by an enemy air raid one night in October 1940.

DOVE GOODS

During the years 1862-67 the LB&SCR acquired 30 standard Craven passenger 2-4-0s. Twelve were built at Brighton Works, Beyer Peacock & Co supplied 12 more, and six came from Dubs & Co. The latter were unpopular with Brighton men who worked

them on fast main-line services, and in September 1881 all six were transferred to Hastings. There, after a while, they spent most of their time on secondary goods duties. The nickname they acquired, however, DOVE GOODS, would appear to be a corruption of DUBS GOODS (qv)—and, despite their relegation from main-line express duties, the DOVE GOODS lasted longest of their class. No 459, the ultimate survivor, was withdrawn in October 1895.

DREADNOUGHTS

In 1878, during his seventh year as CME to the LNWR, F.W. Webb converted an old Trevithick 6-foot single into a two-cylindered compound. Four years later, encouraged by the experiment, he built his first new compound, a 2-2-2-0 named *Experiment*, and 29 more were added by 1884. Webb's next 2-2-2-0 compound design, consisting of 40 locomotives, left Crewe in 1884-88. The

The largest pre-Grouping **DREADNOUGHTS** were these L&YR 4-6-0s. No 1515 was one of the first batch, which was shopped from Horwich Works in 1908. This loco suffered comparatively early withdrawal in August 1925, and although the design was further developed by the L&YR and LMSR during the 1920s, only one, No 50455, reached BR stock. *Author's Collection*

driving wheels were 3 inches smaller at 6 ft 3 in, but the boiler and heating surface were much larger. Heavy on coal and maintenance, but undeniably powerful, these engines soon became known as DREADNOUGHTS. Next, in 1889-90, designed for express work and equipped with 7 ft 1 in driving wheels, came 10 2-2-2-0s of the 'Teutonic' Class. Almost inevitably, they were known as the LARGE DREADNOUGHTS. One might have thought that a naval connotation was out of order here, for nine of the 10 LARGE DREADNOUGHTS built were, in fact, named after White Star liners. Still, these locomotives, too, were successful, all of which persuaded Webb, fallaciously as it happened, to build even bigger compounds. See also SHOOTING GALLERIES.

The next DREADNOUGHTS came from the GNR. During 1889-90 Doncaster Works turned out, at Patrick Stirling's behest, 10 powerful 0-4-4Ts for Metropolitan and London suburban traffic. Instantly successful, 19 more were built in 1891-95. The locomotive's sturdy appearance doubtless inspired the nickname DREADNOUGHTS. The prototype engine, No 766, was withdrawn as the last survivor in February 1927.

In 1908 another DREADNOUGHT came on the scene, when George Hughes, concerned to meet ever increasing loads on L&YR express passenger services, designed his first 4-6-0. Four-cylindered, it had 6 ft 3 in coupled wheels, the boiler was saturated, and a Belpaire firebox and Joy's valve gear were fitted. The class was increased to 20 by March 1909, but alas, teething troubles were formidable, and a decision was made to rebuild them in superheated form, and with Walschaerts valve gear. Unfortunately the eruption of the First World War postponed operation of the plan until 1921, in which year the L&YR also achieved its long-sought amalgamation with the LNWR, and a new series of DREADNOUGHTS began to emerge from Horwich Works. These were equipped with a new type of tender which held 6 tons of coal and 3,000 gallons of water; the working weight thus now rose to 119 tons. In the event, the performance of the new DREADNOUGHTS so transformed events that the LMSR saw fit to add 41 more to the class over the years 1923-25. Under W.A. Stanier's rationalisation policy, however, the DREADNOUGHTS were given short shrift. Withdrawals commenced in 1934, and the last, BR No 50455, went in October 1951.

DROMEDARIES

James Manson's first goods engine design for the G&SWR produced 18 Class '160' 0-6-0s, all built at Kilmarnock in 1897-99. The Manson chimney and rather high cab gave the engines such a humpbacked appearance that they promptly acquired the nickname DROMEDARIES. They were, however, very popular with enginemen, and specialised in working the G&SWR's 'Long Road Goods' between Glasgow and Carlisle. Four were rebuilt in 1926 with the X2 boiler and Whitelegg cab, but it was an unrebuilt one, LMS No 17193, which lived longest, to April 1933.

DRUMMOND'S BABY
See BUTTERFLIES.

DUBS GOODS

These were 0-6-0 goods engines, basically designed by H. Smellie for the G&SWR, but amended and given domes by his successor, James Manson. Dubs & Co built 20 of them in 1892. Vacuum brakes were fitted, and, very popular with Sou' Western men, the 0-6-0s were known as the DUBS GOODS. The LMSR rebuilt three with Whitelegg boilers in 1924-25, and in this form they lasted until 1932. See also DOVE GOODS.

DUKEDOGS

A class of 29 GWR i/c 4-4-0s built in 1936-39, their nickname arose from the fact that the frames came from 'Bulldog' 4-4-0s, while the cabs came from the scrapped 'Dukes' which the new locomotives were meant to replace. The DUKEDOGS did their best work on the Cambrian main line, until 2-6-0s and 'Manors' were allowed to replace them during the Second World War. Withdrawals commenced in 1948, and a sole survivor, No 9017, entered Bluebell Railway stock in June 1962. Its name, *Earl of Berkeley*, though allotted by the GWR, was never carried until the engine came to Sheffield Park. Because of a tendency to slip when working hard, the DUKEDOGS were also known in North Wales as GRASSHOPPERS.

DUNALASTAIRS

J.F. McIntosh had only been in office six months as the CR's Locomotive Superintendent when the great competitive racing to the North commenced in 1895. Following Drummond and Lambie's lead, McIntosh responded by designing a class of 4-4-0 which was to achieve immortality as the DUNALASTAIRS, so called after the prototype which emerged from St Rollox Works in January 1896. Fourteen more followed that year, and the locos were an immediate unqualified success; their speed and haulage capacity set completely new standards in British locomotive performance. Second and third DUNALASTAIRS followed. Superheating was introduced, and before the 4-6-0 type entered CR calculations a fourth class was developed to set the seal of success. Meanwhile, McIntosh's designs were appreciated to the full by the Belgian Government, who latterly built 230 4-4-0s based on the working drawing of the CR engines. The last DUNALASTAIR to run on British metals, BR No 54439, was withdrawn in August 1958.

DUNDEE BOGIES

Five 7 ft 2 in 4-4-0s built by Neilson & Co for the CR in 1877 from a design largely influenced by George Brittain, the CR's newly appointed Locomotive Superintendent. Under-boilered, these engines gave disappointing performances on the Carlisle route, and were latterly diverted to working Dundee trains, even after reboiling by Dugald Drummond. Consequently nicknamed DUNDEE BOGIES, the last of these unfortunate locomotives was withdrawn in August 1910.

DUNDEE ROLLERS

An affectionate nickname for Dugald Drummond's lovely little 4-4-0 passenger tanks, 30 of which were built at Cowlairs for the NBR in 1880-84. The first 24 were given NBR place names in the Stroudley/Drummond tradition, but these vanished once Matthew Holmes took over in 1882. In their early days a few worked main-line stopping trains between Dundee and Dunfermline, and no doubt the 'roller' aspect of their nickname came from the little tanks' distinctive solid cast bogies. Whatever, August 1933 saw the last of the Class 'D51s', as they were known on the LNER.

DX

Designed by J. Ramsbottom, the LNWR's Class 'D' express goods 0-6-0s, the 'DXs', formed Crewe's largest mass-produced class: a total of 857 were built during 1858-74. Driving wheels were 5 feet in diameter, and the engines bore distinctive sloping smokebox fronts with drop-down doors. Fifty-four of them bore names when built, but these were removed in 1864, and green livery was changed to black in 1873 in accordance with new LNWR policy. The last of the class was withdrawn in 1902.

In due course Ramsbottom's successor, F.W. Webb, rebuilt 500 'DXs', commencing in 1881, to form a new class of SPECIAL DX. The rebuilt engines were given new boilers and smokeboxes and, possessed of a fast turn of speed, quite a number, fitted with the vacuum brake, worked express duties during the compound era. Gradually they were replaced by Webb 17-inch COAL ENGINES (qv) and his CAULIFLOWERS (qv). The pioneer SPECIAL DX, No 8000, lasted 70 years to 1928, and the final survivor went in 1930.

The Stroudley influence on Dugald Drummond is clear to be seen in this Kittybrewster study of DUNDEE ROLLER No 10461. Classified 'D51' by the LNER, the ex-NBR tank, shopped as No 294 *Clydebank* in 1882, moved to Aberdeen in July 1927, and was withdrawn in October 1932. Note the cowcatchers fitted fore and aft. *Author's Collection*

E

EARLY SHARPS
See LITTLE SHARPS.

EASTLEIGH ARTHURS
The nickname given by SR men to Maunsell's first 10 'King Arthur' 4-6-0s (see also SCOTSMEN) which were built at Eastleigh in 1925. These retained the high-pitched Urie cab, and most of their lives were spent at Salisbury shed, where they were most popular. Their SR numbers were 448-457, and No 30451 *Sir Lamorak* was last to go, in June 1962.

EMERALD QUEEN
During the Second World War a number of ex-LSWR JUBILEE (qv) 0-4-2s were hired by the War Department over the period 1940-43, and No 625 was a particular favourite on the Longmoor Military Railway. Painted green, with tender numerals, and nicknamed EMERALD QUEEN, No 625 was retained for special duties, and frequently hauled the Commandant's saloon. The locomotive was eventually withdrawn by the SR in January 1947.

ENCHANTING MARY
See MARYS.

ENGLANDS
The first 2-4-0s for the GWR's standard gauge were a batch of eight built in 1862 by George England & Co of Hatcham Ironworks, Kent: hence their nickname. The engines were designed by Daniel Gooch, and they carried his usual outside frames and domeless boilers. Despite a current preference for single-wheelers, the ENGLANDS were

EASTLEIGH ARTHUR No 449 *Sir Torre* awaits its next duty at Nine Elms. Beautifully painted and temporarily coupled to a Urie 5,000-gallon tender, this locomotive represented the SR at the 1925 Stockton & Darlington Railway Centenary celebrations. It was withdrawn as BR No 30499 in December 1959. *Steamchest*

supplied for express work. They were rebuilt at Wolverhampton between 1868 and 1883; Sir William Harcourt, the Chancellor of the Exchequer, happened to be visiting Stafford Road Works when No 154 was being rebuilt, in November 1878, and the engine was named *Chancellor* in his honour. In later years the ENGLANDS, now known generally as the CHANCELLORS, reverted to working local services in the West. The last, withdrawn in May 1920, registered 1,300,000 miles. Only two of the class, in fact, failed to reach the one million mark.

ENIGMA

William Martley's first design for the LC&DR, built at Longhedge Works in 1869, was a 2-4-0 with 6-foot driving wheels. Martley himself nicknamed it ENIGMA, for work on it was stopped so often for lack of funds that he marvelled the engine was ever completed! The nickname was ultimately adopted for the class of three locomotives.

EXTRA LARGE BLOOMERS
See BLOOMERS.

FARINGDON GOODS
See BLACK PIGS.

FAT NANCIES
The final superheated version of the LNWR's Class 'G' 0-8-0s, the 'G1s' and 'G2s', were impressive looking engines, what with their extended smokeboxes and the Belpaire fireboxes most ultimately acquired. Strong to boot, they were known in the Manchester area as FAT NANCIES. When the Class 'G1s', 170 in number, were introduced in 1912-18, the LNWR's Traffic Department styled them 'D Superheated'. In due course

This Stafford shed view of ex-LNWR 0-8-0 No 49377 underlines the impressive appearance of the FAT NANCIES, as these engines were known around Manchester. This locomotive was a 1940 'G2' rebuild of No 1055, a Webb Class 'D' compound (Crewe Works No 4283/1902). *Author*

they, and the 60 Class 'G2' engines, became popularly known as SUPER Ds. One of the last batch to enter traffic, 'G2' No 9446, was an LMSR exhibit at the Darlington centenary celebrations of 1925, and the prototype 'G2', No 49395, was eventually preserved.

FIERY MARY
See MARYS.

FINDHORN ENGINE
This Neilson-built 3 ft 6 in 0-4-0T was acquired in 1862 by the Inverness & Aberdeen Junction Railway when the latter took over the working of the Findhorn Railway. Shortly after the HR was formed in June 1865, Stroudley took the odd little box tank into Lochgorm Works for extensive overhaul, whence it resumed its previous duties, until the 3-mile branch from Findhorn to Kinloss was closed in January 1869. Still known to HR men as the FINDHORN ENGINE, the curious little hybrid carried on,

shunting at Inverness, until it was sold for £600 to a private contractor in September 1872.

FIRST DEGREES
All passenger tender locomotives which were designed by Matthew Holmes for the NBR were 4-4-0s, and his 'classic' was a series of 12 '317' Class engines, ordered by NBR Directors in March 1902. Only four had been built at Cowlairs when poor Holmes died, on 4 July 1903. The remainder were, nevertheless, completed before his successor, W.P. Reid, assumed substantive office. Designed to handle heavy traffic on the Aberdeen line, and known, therefore, to NBR men as FIRST DEGREE engines, the '317s' had a comparatively short life thereon, and were widely distributed on less important duties by the time the Grouping arrived in 1923. All entered LNER stock as Class 'D26', but only one, No 9325, saw 1926 in. See also GOURLAY ENGINES.

THE FISH/ FISH ENGINES

This was J.G. Robinson's first 4-6-0 type for the GCR. Fourteen were built in 1902-04, and their design later formed the basis for his celebrated 'Atlantics' (see JERSEY LILIES). The 4-6-0s were designed to work fast fish trains from Grimsby, and although they were quite frequently employed on passenger trains the nickname THE FISH followed them throughout their long lives. The last of these elegant engines was condemned in June 1950. None was ever superheated, and the LNER classification was 'B5'. In the Manchester area Class 'B4' 4-6-0s were also referred to as the FISH ENGINES. See also SMALL WHEELED FISH.

FLANNEL JACKETS

See SPAM CANS.

FLAT IRONS

Forty of these heavy ponderous class of 0-6-4T were built to R.M. Deeley's design at Derby Works in 1907. Long side tanks, extended to the end of the smokebox, held 2,250 gallons of water, and the bunker took $3\frac{1}{2}$ tons of coal. With a working weight of $75\frac{1}{2}$ tons it was found that the locomotives were unsteady, and oscillated at more than moderate speed. Six were sent to the LT&SR when the MR took over that concern in 1911, but they proved less successful than the engines already working there, and were returned to Derby a few years later. Under LMSR auspices two FLAT IRONS were involved in derailments in near succession, after which the class was forbidden to work passenger trains bunker-first. Their inadequacy brought about abandonment of proposals at Derby to build further 0-6-2Ts, and, later, 2-6-2Ts emerged in lieu. The FLAT IRONS, meanwhile, were all withdrawn in 1935-37. In the Manchester area they were also known as BLOCK TANKS.

FLOATING BATTERIES

Five rear-drive 7-foot singles were built by E.B. Wilson & Co in 1848 for the Eastern

A 1934 Kentish Town view of ex-MR FLAT IRON No 2013. It and No 2011 were fitted with the Westinghouse brake in 1912 for trials on the LT&SR Section, but both returned to more normal MR duties a few years later. All 40 of the class were withdrawn in the mid-1930s. *Steamchest*

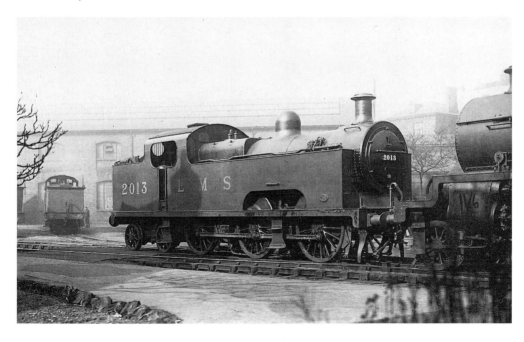

Counties Railway, but proved an acute disappointment on passenger service and were eventually relegated to handling coal trains. These singles did so little work that J.V. Gooch, appointed ECR Locomotive Superintendent in May 1850, incorporated their boilers in the construction of five new goods engines. Solid and outside-framed, with engine and tender weighing 44 tons, the new 0-6-0s were commonly referred to as FLOATING BATTERIES. All were rebuilt in 1867-70 by Robert Sinclair, and the lot were eventually broken up in 1884.

FLYERS
This nickname was given to the GWR's well-loved 0-4-2Ts and 2-4-0Ts, and was also lavished on the L&YR's Class 'J4' 4-4-0s.

FLYING BEDSTEADS
See SQUARE CABS.

FLYING FLOGGER
This 2-2-2 tender engine, owned by the Shrewsbury & Chester Railway and built by Jones & Potts in 1852 for £2,000, had 6 ft 6 in driving wheels, and was one of the first standard gauge locomotives owned by the GWR, once the latter took over the S&CR in 1854. The loco was rebuilt at Wolverhampton in 1860, still as a 2-2-2, but with smaller driving wheels and outside frames. It was eventually taken out of stock in 1873.

FLYING PIGS
This unkind nickname was bestowed upon H.G. Ivatt's Class '4MT' 2-6-0s, the last LMS design to appear before nationalisation. Some 162 were built from 1947 onwards, and the first 50 were fitted with a double chimney. This did little to enhance their distinctly outlandish appearance, though all 50 were later restored to single chimney condition. Known alternatively as WARTHOGS, these locomotives had very high footplates, well clear of the cylinders, and the cab sides stopped short of tender footplate level. On the other hand, their enclosed cabs and tender shields

The subject of several uncomplimentary nicknames, H.A. Ivatt's Class '4MT' 2-6-0s represented the LMSR's last fling before nationalisation. Seen at Colwick in 1959, No 43012 reminds us of why the first 50 were known as FLYING PIGS. *Author*

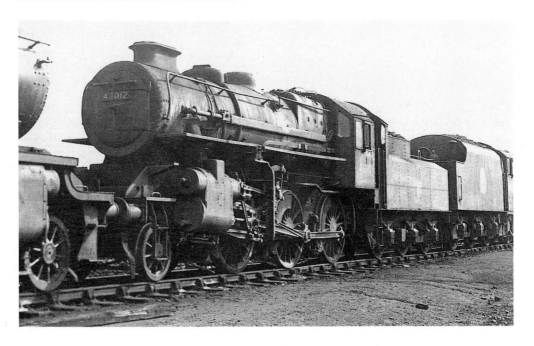

offered welcome shelter to locomen when working in more exposed areas. No 43106, withdrawn from Lostock Hall shed in July 1968, now resides on the Severn Valley Railway.

The type was also known to many as CLODHOPPERS, and Somerset & Dorset Section men referred to them as DOODLEBUGS. See also UTILITIES for an SR version.

FOLKSTONES

When the SER received delivery of 10 i/c 4-2-0 express engines of the latest Crampton type in 1851 from Robert Stephenson & Co, the Board was so proud of its latest acquisition that it arranged for the prototype, No 134, to appear at the International Exhibition at Hyde Park. The locomotive was named *Folkstone* (sic) for the occasion, and the whole class came to be known as such. Nine were rebuilt by Cudworth as more conventional 2-4-0s in 1868-69, and the last of the class vanished in 1892. They must have been good engines, for James Stirling reboilered them a second time in 1880-81.

FOLKESTONE TANKS

Just before J. Cudworth retired from SER service in September 1876 he decided to replace the rather ancient BULLDOGS (qv), then working on the Folkestone Harbour branch, with three purpose-built 0-6-0Ts. His successor, R. Mansell, took up the design, adding enclosed cabs and lengthening the side tanks; the resultant locomotives, costing £1,785 each, entered traffic at Folkestone in March 1877. A reliable, if unspectacular, decade and a half of service on harbour duties was unduly enlivened in October 1886, when No 152 was impounded by HM Customs. A quantity of brandy was found concealed in the engine's bunker, and the train crew were placed under arrest. Three of James Stirling's Class 'R' 0-6-0Ts, built that year, assumed their numbers 152-54, and a new class of FOLKESTONE TANKS entered railway folklore.

FOLLIES

A nickname applied to Joseph Beattie's three 'Eagle' Class o/c 2-4-0s not long after Nine Elms Works delivered them, new, to Exeter early in 1863. All three came a cropper, one way or another, within a year or two, and, regarded warily by Exeter men, they were known locally as the FOLLIES. None lasted beyond February 1886.

FOOTBALLERS

These represented the final batch of 25 'Sandringham' Class 'B17' 4-6-0s (see also SANDIES), built for the LNER in 1935-37. In this instance the normal practice of adopting names of well-known country seats was abandoned, and the engines were named instead after Football Association clubs whose grounds lay in LNER territory. The usual curved nameplate was employed, but underneath there appeared an 8½-inch replica of half a football. This was flanked by enamelled plates which bore the Club colours. Naturally, this bold initiative aroused great public interest, and the locomotives were soon nicknamed FOOTBALLERS. Those which served later on the former GCR main line attracted the additional nickname of OLD SCHOOL TIES. The first four FOOTBALLERS were named after the FA Cup semi-finalists for the year 1935-36. The last to be scrapped, in August 1960, was No 61668 *Bradford City*.

FOURTEEN WHEELERS.

This proud, and self-explanatory, nickname was coined by LB&SCR men when L.B. Billinton's 'Baltic' tank, No 327 *Charles C. Macrae*, entered service in September 1915 after one year of intensive, and instructive, trials. Only one more was built before the First World War intervened, but five more, modified in design, were shopped from Brighton Works in 1921-22. A decade later the need for these powerful tanks receded as SR electrification advanced, and R.E.L. Maunsell implemented a bold decision to rebuild all seven as 4-6-0 tender engines. This project was completed by April 1936, and in another imaginative touch all except *Remembrance* were named after pre-Grouping locomotive engineers. The last survivor, No

Shopped by R. Stephenson & Co on 13 May 1937, and named *Manchester City*, LNER FOOT-BALLER No 2870 was renamed *Tottenham Hotspur* a fortnight later—to enable the locomotive to be exhibited at Hoe Street, Walthamstow. Four months after that, No 2870 was streamlined, for the purpose of handling the LNER's new high speed 'East Anglian', and was renamed *City of London* in the process! *Author's Collection*

This 1914 Brighton Works photograph of No 327 *Charles C. Macrae*, the first of the LB&SCR's six 'Baltic' tanks, exudes the great pride Brighton men took in their FOURTEEN WHEELERS. Who could have guessed that the 4-6-4T would finish up, 21 years later, as No 2327 *Trevithick*, a Southern Railway 'N15X' 4-6-0 tender engine! *Southern Railway*

32331 *Beattie*, was withdrawn in July 1957, but all seven engines completed well over one million miles each.

FOWLER'S GHOST

When London's first Underground line, that of the Metropolitan Railway between Paddington and Farringdon Street, was opened in 1863, the resident Engineer, John Fowler, aspired to solve the problem of tunnel fumes by using steam which was generated in a locomotive boiler by firebricks previously brought to white heat. To achieve this end Fowler designed a remarkable, albeit very handsome, 2-4-0 tender engine, which R. Stephenson & Co built at a total cost of £4,518. Alas, it failed to pass a 7½-mile test on GWR metals, and, known subsequently as FOWLER'S GHOST, it passed unlamented into railway history. Rather sadly, by February 1865 the Metropolitan Railway was advertising it for sale—'either entire, or in parts'.

FREAKS

The GWR's first engines were delivered in 1837, and up to 1854 the Company's entire stock consisted of broad gauge locomotives. The first to run was *Vulcan*, a 2-2-2 supplied by Tayleur & Co, and one of 18 such engines provided by five different firms. Built largely to Brunel's specification, but differing considerably in individual detail, these locos were not a success; dubbed FREAKS, they got GWR broad gauge operations off to a poor start. Fortunately, Gooch's 'Star' and 'Firefly' Classes of 2-2-2 arrived in time to point the GWR in the right direction. Though 10 of the FREAKS soon vanished from the scene, the remaining eight survived in rebuilt form for 30 more years.

FRENCHMEN

G.J. Churchward's accession as CME in May 1902 was a highly significant event in GWR annals. Three 4-6-0s, prototypes of the 'Saint' Class to be, emerged from Swindon by December 1903 as a measure of Churchward's search for stronger, more efficient express locomotives, and embodied much of the simplicity of American design. Yet Churchward was also aware that de Glehn 'Atlantics' were putting up magnificent performances in France. Thus he took the unusual step of persuading his Board to order three French machines for comparative trials on GWR metals. One can imagine the interest with which GWR men viewed the FRENCHMEN, as they were soon known. All built by Société Alsace of Belfort, they yielded Churchward much valuable information, and, rebuilt as experience dictated, they undoubtedly paved the way for his immortal 'Star' Class, the first of which, No 40 *North Star*, was shopped in 4-4-2 form from Swindon in 1906. The FRENCHMEN continued working, meanwhile, and all completed over 700,000 miles before retiring in 1926-28.

FRIDAY NIGHT

An affectionate nickname which was bestowed by GWR men on 'Star' Class 4-6-0 No 4014 *Knight of the Bath*!

FROGGIES

During September-December 1919 the War Department loaned 50 GCR-type ROD (qv) 2-8-0s to the CR. Though not popular with Caledonian men because of their right-hand drive, the RODs handled a deal of coal and steel trains throughout Central Scotland. Known to CR men as FROGGIES, they were latterly placed in a store at Gretna, before being distributed to the LNER, Australia and China during 1925-27.

FROTHBLOWERS

See CRABS.

G

GADGETS

See CRYSTAL SETS.

GALLOPING ALICE

In 1895 Beyer Peacock sold a surplus 2-6-0

GALLOPING ALICE, the M&SWJR's Beyer Peacock purchase of 1895, must have made a glorious sight one day in the late 1920s, when, as GWR No 24, she was conscripted to replace a failed 'King'—and handled an eastbound express as far as Swindon! *Steamchest*

tender engine, built for South America, to the M&SWJR. With an unusually low running-plate and shallow splashers over its 4-foot coupled wheels, the loco, numbered 14, proved so satisfactory on freight duties that a second, No 16, was ordered from Beyer Peacock in 1897. Known as GALLOPING ALICE for her prowess in handling heavy ballast trains, No 16 was also nicknamed BLACK ALICE because of the thick black smoke she belched when tackling gradients. Then, in July 1923, ALICE became No 24 in GWR stock. Rebuilt in 1925, she handled local pick-up freight work between Swindon and Bristol until withdrawal came in July 1930. Before that critical date, however, the locomotive had its moment of fame—when No 6003 *King George IV* failed one day west of Swindon, GALLOPING ALICE was commandeered to haul the express as far as that station!

GALLOPING SAUSAGE
See HUSH HUSH.

THE GARRATT
Although the LMSR later employed 33 Garratt engines in its own right, *the* GARRATT, in LNER men's eyes, was the 178-ton monster which was turned out, at Gresley's direction, by Beyer Peacock in 1925. The only Garratt on the LNER, and the first to be built for a British main-line company, No 2395 was also the most powerful engine in the British Isles. With three cylinders at each end she could generate the combined effort of the two LNER 'O4' 2-8-0s, and, in fact, replaced same when she took up duties banking coal trains up Worsborough Incline, a distance of 3½ miles at 1 in 40. Firing her, though, was a heavy job for one man. In 1949-50, and again in 1955, the LNER Garratt, now BR No 69999, was tried out on the Lickey Incline. On that territory, however, the massive engine was neither successful nor popular. It was finally withdrawn in December 1955.

GATESHEAD INFANT

This nickname was proudly bestowed by NER men when No 532, Wilson Worsdell's first 'Atlantic', was shopped from Gateshead Works in November 1903, the largest and heaviest 4-4-2 of her time. Nine more followed by 1904, and all were immediately put to work on the heaviest expresses between York and Edinburgh; No 532, in fact, worked the down 'Flying Scotsman' from York when just one week old. Then, as employment of Gresley 'Pacifics' increased, NER 'Atlantics' began to play a less important role. In 1943 it was decided that they were no longer fit for main-line traffic; the GATESHEAD INFANT, first to go, was withdrawn in January 1943.

GENERALS

It was rare indeed for modern freight locomotives to be given names, but when 25 Class 'C' NBR 0-6-0s returned home from service overseas during the First World War they were endowed with suitably commemorative names. As 14 of them bore the names of prominent military figures, such as *Foch*, *Joffre*, *Petain*, etc, they became known as the GENERALS. The LNER classified them 'J36', and one, BR No 65243, has been preserved on its home ground as NBR No 673 *Maude*.

GEORDIES

This nickname was applied, somewhat illogically, by LC&DR men to six GNR 2-2-2s which were borrowed for six months from 1 November 1860 to assist in opening the LC&DR's Western extension. A similar solecism occurred when the SE&CR were lent 15 GNR 2-4-0s over 50 years later! During that acute shortage of motive power on the SE&CR in 1913 the borrowed engines actually carried the letters 'SE&CR' on their tenders. All were returned north with thanks in 1915.

GERMANS

Because a British locomotive manufacturer

When NER Class 'V' 'Atlantic' No 532 was shopped from Gateshead in 1903, with the same boiler girth (5 ft 6 in) as the GNR's 'Large Atlantic' No 251, NER men were so impressed by the size of the locomotive that they christened her the GATESHEAD INFANT. Precursor of a 20-strong class, No 532 became the first LNER 'C6' to be withdrawn, in January 1943. *Author's Collection*

could not guarantee delivery by August 1914, the SE&CR switched an order for 19 Class 'L' 4-4-0s to a German firm, A. Borsig of Tegel. Borsig duly commenced delivery on 24 May 1914, when two 'Ls' arrived, partially dismantled, at Dover. Three more followed on 26 May, and the remainder arrived on 11 June. Numbered 772-781, the 10 locos were prepared for service at Ashford Works by German fitters, who also travelled on the footplate when trial runs were made, and only just got back to Germany before hostilities commenced on 4 August 1914. During the ensuing war the Class 'Ls', totalling 22 in number, handled heavy troop trains with ease. The class remained intact until 1956, but by 1961 all had gone; the last, No 780, held out until July of that year.

GINX'S BABIES
A series of six o/c 4-4-0s which were designed by T. Bouch for the Stockton & Darlington Railway in 1871-72, their duties lay in hand-ling passenger trains on the S&D's steeply graded section between Tebay and Darlington. The generous proportions of these engines earned them the (locally relevant) nickname GINX'S BABIES, and it was said that they could run at 60 mph with a 14-coach load. No 1269 of the species was exhibited during the Stockton & Darlington Jubilee celebrations of 1875. All gave trouble, however, and the class was rebuilt, with slide valves and in 2-4-0 form, in 1879-80. Six similar 4-4-0s were built, still to Bouch's design, by the NER in 1874. Constructed at Darlington, all were again rebuilt as 2-4-0s, but were cut up to a man in 1914.

GLASSHOUSES
When the SE&CR was formed on 1 January 1899, reliable passenger locomotives were at a premium. To meet the crisis, five new 4-4-0s, offered by Neilson Reid & Co of Glasgow, were accepted at a cost of £3,300 each. Part of an unrequited order for the GNSR, the

GLASSHOUSE No 676, though built initially by Neilson & Co for the GNSR, heads a SE&CR express train through Beckenham Junction as to the manner born. *Steamchest*

engines were styled in the unmistakeable fashion of that Scottish railway. They were of neat appearance, though their left-hand drive proved to be unpopular with SE&CR men, who were long accustomed to driving from the right. Extremely roomy cabs, with twin glass side windows and roof ventilators, soon earned them the nickname GLASSHOUSES. Sometimes they were referred to as ABERDEENS, or HERRINGS, because of their close connection with the Granite City. The last was withdrawn in 1927, long before many of their Scottish counterparts (LNER Class 'D40s') perished.

GOBBLERS

A group of 30 Class 'M15' 2-4-2Ts which were introduced on the GER by T.W. Worsdell in 1884-86. The Joy's valve gear with which these engines were fitted was unsuitable for their purpose, and led to a very heavy and rapid coal consumption; thus, GOBBLERS they became. Wordsell's successor, James Holden, built 10 more in 1886, this

time with Stephenson's valve gear—and the problem was solved. Unfortunately, the nickname persisted. The 30 original locos were later rebuilt along the same lines, and the class became 'F4' under LNER auspices. Busy active engines, the last was not withdrawn until May 1958. During the Second World War many had their chimneys reduced, for, in the event of London Transport's electricity supply being disrupted by enemy action, the LNER had undertaken to work the Metropolitan line, with its attendant restricted tunnel clearances.

GOURLAY ENGINES

Railwaymen have long memories, and this nickname evokes memories of the Elliot Junction disaster long after the tragedy occurred on 28 December 1906. The NBR express engine involved, No 324, one of Holmes's Class 'K' 4-4-0s (see FIRST DEGREES), was running tender-first that snowbound evening when it collided with a stationary train. The fireman was killed and

GOBBLER. No 663 was one of the original 30 Class 'M15' GER tanks which generated the nickname. Classified 'F4' by the LNER, it was an early casualty in September 1925. *Steamchest*

the ultimate death roll was 22, but driver Gourlay survived to face trial on grounds of culpable homicide. Suspicions were that Gourlay had been drinking, though many still think the driver was unfortunate to receive a five-month prison sentence. Whatever, the stigma attached itself to Holmes's '317' 4-4-0s, later LNER Class 'D26', and almost to the end of their days in the mid-1920s these fine locomotives were referred to by some as the GOURLAY ENGINES.

GOUROCK BOGIES

The CR's answer to the G&SWR's WEE BOGIES (qv) in the grim competition which was waged by both Companies for Clyde steamer traffic, the GOUROCK BOGIES were Drummond-designed i/c 4-4-0s, with coupled wheels of only 5 ft 9 in diameter. Twelve were built at St Rollox between 1888 and 1891, and were an instant success; though, of course, the CR route to Gourock was less demanding than that of the G&SWR. Three did not survive to wear LMS colours, and those remaining were withdrawn by 1930. These engines were also known as the COAST BOGIES.

GRASSHOPPERS

A grasshopper is a light, nimble, rather spare creature. So, too, was the elementary locomotive which Timothy Hackworth built at Wylam Colliery engine shops in 1813. The boiler had a single return flue, the two cylinders were vertical, and power was transmitted through longitudinal levers to a geared shaft. Even though the locomotive proved to be too heavy for the cast iron plate rails then in use, it soon attracted the nickname GRASSHOPPER.

So, too, nearly a century later, did 40 MT 4-4-0s Dugald Drummond designed for the LSWR in 1901-02. With many semi-fast and light freight services to handle, the Company found ample use for these nippy little Class 'K10s'. Like all Drummond 4-4-0s, the LSWR GRASSHOPPERS were neat and attractive, albeit rather slight in appearance. They saw wide service in the LSWR's Western Section, and during the Second World

War one or two wandered off elsewhere in the UK. Withdrawals commenced in January 1947, but 31 of the species still survived to enter BR stock. The last, No 384, was not broken up until August 1951. Meanwhile, an enlarged version of these MT 4-4-0s was introduced by Drummond in 1903, and the 'K10s' became known thereafter as SMALL HOPPERS. The new LARGE HOPPERS, officially classified 'L11', were even better than the 'K10s'; 40 were built at Nine Elms between 1903 and 1907, and in addition to handling troop and naval specials during the First World War they were used for fast passenger services on the busy Portsmouth line. Unlike Drummond's GREYHOUNDS (qv), however, they were never superheated. Despite that, all 40 entered BR stock in 1948. Withdrawals commenced seriously in 1951, and in November of that year the last two survivors were scrapped.

The first LB&SCR tender engines to have leading bogies were also nicknamed GRASSHOPPERS. These were Billinton's 'B2' Class 4-4-0s, 25 of which, all bearing names, were turned out by Brighton Works in 1895-97 (see also BRASSBACKS). Officially they were styled 'B Bogies', but because of their pronounced vulnerability in springing, Brighton men, who heartily detested them, dubbed them GRASSHOPPERS. Nevertheless, despite their shortcomings the 'B2s' registered high annual mileages, and only one failed to exceed one million miles. All were rebuilt as Class 'B2X' before the Grouping, but none survived beyond 1933. See also DUKEDOGS.

GREAT 'A'

This was a long-boilered, rear-driving 4-2-0 with a haystack firebox which was built by R. Stephenson & Co in 1845 (Works No 494) for the York & North Midland Railway. As the engine bore the letter 'A' on the second ring of its boiler it was invariably referred to by enginemen as 'Engine A' or the GREAT 'A'. It probably graduated as NER No 290 in due course, but nothing is known of its ultimate disposal. The locomotive was used in the Gauge Commission Trials of 1845.

GREEN BOGIES

Thomas Parker, Locomotive Superintendent of the MS&LR, produced 31 new Class '2' and '2A' i/c 4-4-0s during 1887-94. Handsome engines, they were a complete departure from previous Gorton practice in having inside frames. The prototype, No 561, entered MS&LR service after being featured at the Manchester Jubilee Exhibition. At that time MS&LR passenger trains were generally modest in nature, so perhaps the new 4-4-0s' average coal consumption of 24 lbs per mile was not so startling as it sounds. Classified 'D7', all 31 entered LNER stock, whence, under initial LNER painting policy, they qualified, as passenger locomotives, for the standard green livery. Like many other LNER types they were obliged, however, to accept black livery with red lining from June 1928 onwards. But during these four carefree years they were known to ex-GCR men, especially those at Immingham shed, as the GREEN BOGIES. December 1939 saw the last of them, when No 5704 was withdrawn.

GREENOCK BOGIES

Here was the other side of fierce competition between the CR and the G&SWR for Scottish west coast traffic (see GOUROCK BOGIES). In 1882-85 Hugh Smellie, the G&SWR's Locomotive Superintendent, built 24 i/c 4-4-0s. Specifically designed to handle Greenock line traffic, they were consequently nicknamed GREENOCK BOGIES by Sou' Western men. Typical Smellie locomotives, they had domeless boilers, and, classified '1P', all but two entered LMSR stock in 1923. Meanwhile, the nickname of these 4-4-0s changed to WEE BOGIES as Smellie's successor, James Manson, brought out his 4-4-0 i/c version in 1895. The first 10 of these were built by Dubs & Co, and 15 more were added by the same firm in 1899. Fine engines, with 6 ft 1 1/4 in coupled wheels,

Despite their stovepipe chimneys, the MS&LR GREEN BOGIES were a handsome vindication of Thomas Parker's belief in single frames. No 5684, seen here as LNER Class 'D7', was built at Gorton in 1891, and, rebuilt with a Belpaire firebox in 1912, was withdrawn from New Holland in July 1939.
Steamchest

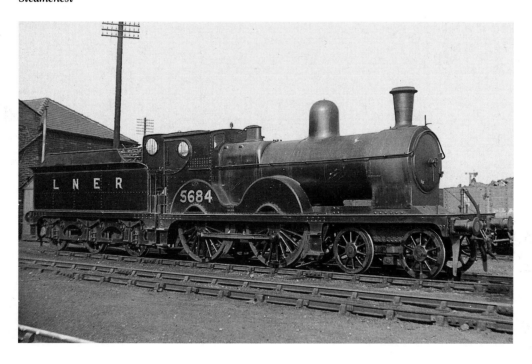

they were a great success, and, known affectionately in turn as the GREENOCK BOGIES, they monopolised traffic in the Greenock area for years to follow. Some trains were even advertised as 'No Luggage', so keen was the G&SWR to outspeed its Caley rival! Latterley, all Manson 'Bogies' passed into LMSR ownership, but by 1932 stringency in eliminating small non-standard classes saw to their demise.

GREEN TANKS

These were five class 'H16' 4-6-2Ts which were designed by Robert Urie in 1921 for shunting duties at the LSWR's Feltham marshalling yard. Used occasionally on suburban passenger trains, these tanks were given a green livery by the SR, as opposed to the somewhat similar 4-8-0Ts which were painted black (see BLACK TANKS). Almost inevitably the 'H16s' became known as the GREEN TANKS. All were withdrawn in 1962.

GREYBACKS

When, in 1922, R. Billinton decided to rebuild, and superheat, 12 of his 'B4' 4-4-0s to from a new Class 'B4X', the Grouping was imminent. As a result, the locomotives were not given the usual LB&SCR umber livery, but were turned out from Brighton Works simply in shop grey. The nickname GREYBACKS soon came their way. None too distinguished in performance, the first 'B4Xs' were withdrawn in the mid-1930s. The remainder, lingering on to perform modest duties, followed suit in 1951. See also BUSTERS.

Also known as GREYBACKS, for rather less complimentary reasons (for the term means 'louse' in the Scottish vernacular), W.Pickersgill's first 4-6-0 design for the CR pursued equally undistinguished careers. St Rollox built six in 1916-17, but they proved disappointingly sluggish in performance. Some measure of LMSR difficulties in early Grouping days is indicated by the fact that 20 more were added to the class in 1925-26. Latterly, the class '60s', as they were officially known, were entrusted mainly with mixed traffic, and by 1953 the last had gone.

GREYBACK. Built by Sharp Stewart & Co in 1901 as LB&SCR Class 'B4' No 72 *Sussex*, and rebuilt as a 'B4X' in 1924, SR No 2072 is seen here at Redhill in 1948. Note the Weir pump on the footplate. Stored at Eastbourne in 1951, the locomotive was finally withdrawn in December of that year, with a cumulative mileage of 1,240,408. *Steamchest*

GREY GHOST
See HUSH HUSH.

GREYHOUNDS
An improved class of i/c 4-4-0, designed by Dugald Drummond for the LSWR, the first 30 were built by Dubs & Co in 1899-1900. They cost £2,945 each, and it is interesting to note that six other firms who were invited to tender quoted prices ranging from £3,117 to £3,800. One more, No 773, was built specially, at a cost of £3,200, by Dubs & Co for display at the Glasgow Exhibition of 1901. It was so beautifully finished that a repaint was not required until 4½ years later. During the years 1899 and 1901 a further 35 were built at Nine Elms Works. Reliable and free-running engines, the 'T9s', as they were classified, could be flogged mercilessly on express passenger duties. But, like Ivatt's GNR 'Atlantics', their true worth was only revealed when they were superheated. R.W.

Urie and the SR attended to this in the 1920s, and it was then that the GREY-HOUNDS really earned their nickname. Popular to the last, all saw 1950 in before surrendering. Fortunately, one, No 120, has been preserved, albeit in superheated form, but decked in full LSWR livery.

GUNBOATS
These nine 0-4-4Ts, designed for the SER by R. Mansell, incorporated a surprise reversion to many obsolescent Ashford Works features, such as outside frames and safety valves on domes. Built rapidly at Ashford between January and May 1878, these tanks, Mansell hoped, would impress the SER Directors. Nicknamed GUNBOATS because of their sharp bark when working hard, the tanks performed with reasonable success on London suburban services, but were replaced ten years later by larger, more powerful 'Q' Class 0-4-4Ts. All the GUNBOATS had vanished by 1891.

Rebuilt GREYHOUND No 30117 finished up with a cumulative mileage of 1,982,396. Part of that was earned piloting SR SPAM CANS (qv), as seen here at Upney in August 1952. *Author*

HAMWORTHY BUSES
See IRONCLADS.

HASTINGS
A series of 10 i/c 2-4-0s with an unusually short wheelbase, built for the SER at Ashford Works in 1853-54. They were capable useful engines, with a remarkable turn of speed, and promptly excelled themselves on the Hastings branch, hence their nickname. By the 1860s, however, they lost pride of place to the LITTLE MAILS (qv). Four more HASTINGS were built by R. Stephenson & Co in 1854, but, rather less certain in operation than the originals, these were withdrawn in 1870. The original HASTINGS saw another 13 years' service.

HAWKSHAW SINGLES
Of this extensive series of 2-2-2s built for the L&YR during 1847-49, 26 of the 5 ft 9 in variety were built at Miles Platting Works, and Fairbairn & Co contributed 17 more. The same two sources contributed six and four 5 ft 6 in versions, and a final 29 5 ft 10 in engines were added by Bury, Curtis & Kennedy in 1849. All were commonly known as HAWKSHAW SINGLES after the L&YR's Chief Engineer, but as Hawkshaw was not a locomotive designer they should more properly be attributed to W. Jenkins, the Company's Locomotive Superintendent. Most of these engines were rebuilt as 2-4-0s in the late 1860s, but only lasted another 10 years.

HELL FIRE JACKS
Towards the end of the 19th century the introduction of steam sanding aroused a new affection for single wheelers. H. Pollitt's last design for the GCR, for instance, resulted in six Belpaire-fireboxed 4-2-2s being shopped from Gorton Works in 1900. An early duty of the first-built, No 967, was to haul a Royal Special carrying the King of Sweden from Marylebone to Sheffield. Rather prone to slipping, the 4-2-2s were known to GCR men as HELL FIRE JACKS. Robinson rebuilt four with new boilers and superheaters in 1915-19. None survived long after the Grouping, however, and the last of the 7 ft 9 in 'X4s', as they were classified on the LNER, was withdrawn in August 1927.

HERRINGS
See GLASSHOUSES.

HIELMEN
Presumably an abbreviation of 'Hielan' men', this nickname was applied by CR men to six 'River' Class 4-6-0s which were bought from the HR in 1915. Designed by F.G. Smith, these massive engines were built by Hawthorn Leslie & Co of Newcastle, but only two had been delivered to Inverness before the HR's Civil Engineer rejected them as being too heavy for some of his bridges. Sold to the CR, and the direct cause of F.G. Smith's resignation, the six 'Rivers' then assumed CR Nos 938-43. The ultimate irony came after Grouping, when, as LMSR Nos 14756-61, they worked frequently in the Highland Section once a few bridges had been strengthened. The last of the HIELMEN, No 14760, was withdrawn in August 1927.

HIGHFLYERS
Railwaymen loved sure-footed speedy locomotives, and no greater accolade could be bestowed on any express type than to be nicknamed HIGHFLYERS. Thus, with hard running a positive tradition on LNWR West Coast services, some of the earliest types to be so honoured were J. Ramsbottom's 'Problem' and 'Lady of the Lake' 2-2-2s of 1859-65. Fitted with timber-framed tenders in case of accident, these handsome engines ran rather unsteadily at speed. But they served the LNWR well, and the last did not go until 1907.

The nickname HIGHFLYERS was next lavished on Patrick Stirling's beautiful 4-2-2 GNR '8-footers', his only design with outside cylinders and a leading bogie. The first two emerged from Doncaster in 1870, and others

HIGHFLYER. Elegance personified, the GNR's last 'enlarged' 8-foot single, No 1008, emerged from Doncaster Works in April 1895, at a cost of £2,240 for the engine alone. Never rebuilt, it served the GNR faithfully until June 1914. *O.J. Morris*

J.A.F. Aspinall also created a legendary series of HIGHFLYERS, when 20 7 ft 3 in 'Atlantics' were shopped from Horwich Works in 1899. Rather incongruously, they carried tenders which were 'borrowed' from rebuilt Barton Wright 0-6-0s. One of the HIGHFLYERS is seen here leaving York. *Steamchest*

followed to create a class of 53 by 1895, which excelled themselves on main-line express work, particularly during the 'Race to the North' in 1895. Stirling was traditionally much averse to coupled locomotives, and his last batch of six of that year was a bold bid to perpetuate the 'Singles'; but it was patently obvious by then that increasing workloads demanded coupled locomotives. Fortunately, the first GNR HIGHFLYER, No 1, was retained at King's Cross shed after running 1,400,000 miles—and even reappeared on main-line metals in 1938 to run special excursions. She is now resident at the National Railway Museum, York.

Also dubbed HIGHFLYERS were the L&YR's Class 'J4' i/c 4-4-0s, 40 in number, introduced by J.A.F. Aspinall in 1891-94. With 7 ft 3 in driving wheels, they thoroughly earned their keep, and handled most L&YR express work of the time, including Bradford–St Pancras trains as far as Sheffield. G. Hughes rebuilt six with superheaters in 1907-09, and all 40 entered LMSR stock at the Grouping. None survived, however, to greet the dawn of BR in 1948.

The L&YR's next HIGHFLYERS were Aspinall's i/c 'Atlantics'. A first batch of 20, again with 7 ft 3in wheels, was shopped from Horwich Works in 1899. They created enormous interest, and 20 more were added in 1902. The prototype, No 1400, had the largest boiler of any British locomotive of its day, and the class, also known as FLYERS, gained a great reputation amongst L&YR men. Rumour has it that a speed of over 100 mph was recorded on a trial run between Liverpool and Southport in July 1899, but this has never been truly verified. Whatever, all 40 HIGHFLYERS survived the Grouping; then, typical of contemporary LMSR policy, the class was allowed to slip away. Withdrawals commenced in 1926, and the last vanished in November 1933. See also TINIES.

HIKERS

This nickname was applied by Scottish railwaymen to those of J. Holden's ex-GER Class 'B12' 4-4-0s which were fitted with ACFI

ACFI feed water heating apparatus. Built at Stratford Works in 1911, the first five, as LNER Nos 8500-04, found their way to the Aberdeen area in 1931, and there they served admirably on former GNSR territory. Others followed later. The bulky ACFI apparatus, sited on top of the boiler behind the chimney, had already inspired the nickname CAMEL (qv) amongst GER men, and no doubt it was the likeness of the equipment to a hiker's pack which persuaded the Scottish men to dub these locomotives HIKERS. Those of Fowler's LMS BABY AUSTIN (qv) 0-8-0s which also carried ACFI equipment were similarly nicknamed HIKERS further south. An alternative reason for the 'B12s' being known as HIKERS might well be that the locomotives' cabs were so deep that a fireman ferrying coal between tender and firebox was obliged to take one extra step.

Conversely, LMS MT 4-6-0s (see BLACK FIVES) were also known as HIKERS on the Highland Section because of their ability, and willingness, to 'step out'.

HOLE IN THE WALL TANK

In 1891, when T. Parker, Locomotive Superintendent of the MS&LR, began building Class '9C' 0-6-2Ts, the prototype, No 7, was the first British locomotive to introduce the Belpaire firebox. A total of 129 of these useful 5 ft 9 in tanks were built by 1901. One, No 771, was rebuilt by J.G. Robinson in 1915 with a superheater and increased coal and water capacity. Side tanks, extended both vertically and horizontally, were now flush with the front of the smokebox; with an opening provided, as with Gresley's ARDSLEY TANKS (qv), to offer access to the motion, this solitary rebuild became known as the HOLE IN THE WALL TANK. The LNER classified the loco successively as 'N5/2' and 'N5/3', and it was ultimately withdrawn from service in February 1952. In all, 121 'N5' tanks lived to enter BR service.

HORNBIES

H.G. Ivatt's Class '2MT' 2-6-0s, introduced in December 1946, were tidy and highly efficient machines, and 128 of them were built between 1946 and 1953. Their some-what minute proportions, however, aroused some derision at St Margarets shed, Edin-burgh, where men were more accustomed to Gresley's more impressive-looking LNER '3Ks', and there the '2MTs' were referred to, rather slightingly, as HORNBIES.

HUMPIES

Between 1871 and 1881 41 of Sacré's stan-dard shunting 0-6-0STs were turned out at Gorton Works. Known on the MS&LR as Class '18T', they had saddle tanks extending forward to the front of the smokebox, open cabs, wooden brake blocks, and buffer planks. By 1903 they were rebuilt with, amongst other refinements, shorter tanks and enclosed cabs. Because of their inadequate brake power, however, they were confined largely to yard shunting duties, whence they readily acquired the nickname HUMPIES. Three were lent to the Rhymney Railway in 1920 to help ease a shortage there of motive power.

Their braking frailties soon revealed them-selves, though, and all were returned to the GCR within a year. Januuary 1929 saw the last, by now LNER Nos 6475 and 6451, go to the scrapyard.

Four much larger 0-8-4Ts, built for GCR hump shunting in 1908-09, were also known as HUMPIES (see WATH DAISIES). So, too, were some GNR 0-6-0STs when they were employed on duties of a similar nature.

HUMPTY DUMPTIES

J. Holden built 110 of his celebrated 7-foot Class 'T19' 2-4-0s between 1886 and 1897. One, fitted for oil burning, received the name *Petrolea*, itself a rare event in GER history. Twenty-one were rebuilt in 1902-04 with a larger boiler, Belpaire firebox and single-windowed cab; in addition, following earlier Holden tradition, the dome was moved fur-ther forward along the boiler. Front bogie wheels of 3 ft 1 in diameter were hopelessly out of proportion with the 7-foot drivers, and

GER Class 'T19' No 1038, rebuilt at Stratford Works in 1904, is hauling a heavy enough train here, but one can see why these engines were nicknamed HUMPTY DUMPTIES. This particular specimen was withdrawn in 1913. *Steamchest*

the provision of a small tender only aggravated their 'front heavy' appearance. Well-named HUMPTY DUMPTIES, these engines were, in fact, much too heavy in front for superheating, and all 21 finished their days using saturated steam.

Meanwhile, 60 more 'T19s' were rebuilt in 1905-08, this time as 4-4-0s. On this occasion the dome was restored to a central position, though all other dimensions were retained. However, even as LNER Class 'D13s' the nickname HUMPTY DUMPTIES still followed the locos. None the less, the last of the species, No 8039, survived until March 1944.

When one of the 'T19' 2-4-0s, No 1035, was rebuilt as a 4-4-0 in 1905 it ran ex-Works in shop grey for some time. GER men, seizing upon a popular song of the period, promptly dubbed the engine DOLLY GRAY. Superheated, like many others, in March 1918, it served the GER and LNER well right up to May 1943.

HUSH HUSH.

Known as the HUSH HUSH before she even entered service, because of the secrecy which, all through 1929, attended her construction at Darlington Works, Gresley's massive 6 ft 8 in 4-6-4 duly emerged in December 1929. A high-pressure 4-cyl compound, and the first locomotive in the UK to embody streamlining in its design, No 10000, clad in battleship grey, aroused enormous public interest. Many referred to her as the GREY GHOST; some LNER officials dubbed her, rather more facetiously, the FLYING SAUSAGE. Nevertheless, No 10000 was the first experimental British locomotive to be employed in *regular* public service. Alas, her water tube boiler proved to be a major weakness, and in the end Gresley decided to rebuild No 10000 as a 3-cyl simple. Thus she reappeared in 1937, closely resembling Gresley's 'A4' 'Pacific' class, but still retaining her unusual wheel arrangement, still classified LNER 'W1', and still unnamed; it was as well, perhaps, that a

The HUSH HUSH. Ready for action at King's Cross soon after entering traffic in June 1930, No 10000, Gresley's sensational new 4-6-4, retained its dark grey livery all through its high-pressure life. *Author's Collection*

1929 proposal to name Gresley's giant *British Enterprise* was never implemented! Latterly, the locomotive became No 60700 under BR auspices, and worked consistently until withdrawal in June 1959. Intriguingly, tender No 5484, which accompanied the HUSH HUSH at all times until May 1948, is now in use with preserved 'A4' 'Pacific' No 60009 *Union of South Africa*.

I

ILFRACOMBE GOODS

When the LSWR assumed responsibility *circa* 1870 for working the Barnstaple & Ilfracombe Railway's sharply curved and heavily graded line, the Company eventually approached Beyer Peacock & Co for advice. After some typical Beattie (father and son)

procrastination, Beyer supplied three of their standard light 0-6-0s in 1872. The engines carried four-wheeled tenders, but, as they proved to be perfectly satisfactory in service, five more were provided between 1874 and 1880. All eight were employed in the West Country, and soon became known as the ILFRACOMBE GOODS. Five were rebuilt in the late 1880s, and later still, between 1910 and 1918, six of the class were sold by the LSWR, to eke out a few more years of service on sundry Colonel Stephens light railways. In typical Stephens fashion, four of them were given classical names, *Thisbé*, *Juno*, *Pyramus* and *Hesperus*.

IMPROVED DIRECTORS
See DIRECTORS.

INTERMEDIATES
Almost identical in apperance to the GER's HUMPTY DUMPTIES (qv), but much smaller in the driving wheel, the INTERME-

Formerly LSWR ILFRACOMBE GOODS 0-6-0 No 0349, K&ESR No 7 *Rother* leaves Headcorn on a goods train for Frittenden Road. The date is 15 September 1910, a few months after the locomotive was acquired. It served the K&ESR for quarter of a century. *LCGB/Ken Nunn Collection*

DIATES were a class of 100 2-4-0s which were designed by J. Holden and built at Stratford Works in 1892-1902. Easy runners and possessed of excellent acceleration, they wandered all over the GER system on secondary passenger duties, cross-country work and branch duties. The LNER classified them as 'E4' when, still intact in number, they were handed over at the Grouping. In 1935 half a dozen were dispatched to work in North Eastern territory, where icy blasts justified the fitting of new cabs with side windows. Eighteen INTERMEDIATES which survived to January 1940 continued in service until 1954, thanks to a shortage of suitable motive power in East Anglia. Then withdrawals recommenced. BR No 62785, the last to go, in December 1959, was restored to its original condition as GER No 490 at Stratford Works, and can now be seen at the National Railway Museum, York.

Also known as INTERMEDIATES were 12 i/c 4-4-0s, W.P. Reid's first design for the NBR, built at Cowlairs in 1906-07. Their ability to tackle any kind of work endeared them to NBR men's hearts, and all subsequent NBR 4-4-0 designs were firmly based upon them. Later classified 'D32' by the LNER, the last INTERMEDIATE, BR No 62451, was not withdrawn until March 1951.

IRONCLADS

A 2-4-0 design was recommended to SER Directors by John Ramsbottom of the LNWR when he was invited to report on the SER's future motive power requirements. The SER's Locomotive Superintendent, James Cudworth, was not notified of his Directors' inquiry, and was consequently thoroughly displeased; but he agreed, none the less, to assist. Thus, 10 locomotives were ordered from each of Sharp Stewart and Avonside

These IRONCLADS were the popular first design of William Adams for the LSWR, 12 sturdy '46' Class 4-4-0Ts supplied by Beyer Peacock in 1878. Built as here, with coal and water capacities of 1¼ tons and 1,000 gallons, their utility was improved in 1883-86, when all were rebuilt as 4-4-2Ts. Extended bunkers now held 3 tons of coal, and a well tank over the trailing wheels added 650 more gallons of water. All were placed on the Duplicate List by 1905, and No 0379 perished in June 1923. *Author's Collection*

Engine Co, and all were supplied in 1876. They soon became known as RAMSBOTTOM EXPRESS ENGINES, or IRONCLADS, the latter nickname inspired by contemporary public absorption with naval craft developments. Still piqued, Cudworth resigned in September 1876; whereafter the SER Chairman's son Alfred Watkins, began his short and disastrous career. Cudworth, however, must have smiled to himself later still, when the much vaunted IRONCLADS proved a grievous disappointment, and had to be replaced on Continental expresses by his own MAILS (qv). The IRONCLADS were subsequently moved around the SER system, but remained steadfastly unpopular with locomen. Though reboilered during 1888-91, all were withdrawn by June 1906.

Also destined to acquire the same nickname was a series of 12 4-4-0 passenger tanks constructed by Beyer Peacock & Co in 1878. Costing £1,995 apiece, they constituted William Adams's first design for the LSWR. Known officially as the '46' Class, they were more frequently referred to as IRONCLADS because of their robust construction and four-square appearance. Though some teething troubles required resolution they performed quite creditably, and certainly widely, on the LSWR system. Two, sub-shedded latterly at Hamworthy Junction, acquired local distinction as the HAMWORTHY BUSES. In due course all of Adams's IRONCLADS except two entered SR service, and the last in traffic, No 0375, was retired from the Swanage branch in July 1925.

The Ironclads of the Royal Navy must certainly have gripped the public imagination. Twenty GER 4-4-0s, designed by William Adams not long before he left Stratford for LSWR pastures, were built in 1876-77 by Dubs & Co and R.&W. Hawthorn. Sturdy o/c engines, they, too, attracted the nickname. Intended for express passenger duties, they proved, however, to be much too heavy for that purpose, and were all diverted latterly to handling fast goods and cattle trains. Their driving wheels were of 6 ft 1 in diameter, and the engine itself weighed 45 tons. Hardly surprisingly, all were scrapped between 1894 and 1897.

One last prolific class earned the nickname IRONCLADS when W. Barton Wright, in the course of renewing practically the whole L&YR stock, had 280 0-6-0 goods engines, identical to a Kitson design on the Taff Vale Railway, built in 1887; their solid and uncompromising bearing soon invited the popular nickname. Later 230 of the class were rebuilt as 0-6-0STs by J.A.F.Aspinall, Wright's successor, during 1891-1900. The saddle tanks, known consequently as the CONVERTED TANKS (qv), were so robust that one of them, No 52044, was the last L&YR engine, and the oldest locomotive in BR service, when it was withdrawn in May 1959. Formerly L&YR No 957, it can be seen now on the Keighley & Worth Valley Railway. Many of the unrebuilt IRONCLADS continued in very popular service in the LNWR area. Tough and well respected, their hard work in the South Lancashire coalfields earned them the nickname WIGAN PIGS.

IRON LUNGS

This rather sardonic nickname was applied to the AUSTERITY (qv) 2-8-0s which were built to Ministry of Supply design and introduced in February 1943. Despite their spartan appearance, these engines rendered yeoman service during Second World War years, and once BR absorbed a final 533 early in 1949 they could be found working on all regional main lines except the Southern.

JACKOS

This nickname was frequently applied to shunting engines by men of BR's Midland and Western Regions.

JACOB

This was the nickname which was given to a solitary CR 0-6-0ST, built by Neilson & Co in 1873. Possibly built originally for export, and left on Neilson's hands, this very power-

Why CR No 141 earned the nickname JACOB remains something of a mystery. But the ruggedly built 0-6-0ST, though falling heir to two Duplicate numbers latterly, served the Scottish company well. *Steamchest*

ful locomotive worked the Cuilhill yard on the Monkland Canal for some time, then became involved in the construction of the Oban line. Its hard-working life culminated in Duplicate Listing in 1899, and again in 1901, and JACOB was withdrawn as No 1516 in 1907.

JAZZERS

A railway world which had seen little development during the First World War years was duly enlivened in 1920, when Doncaster produced the first British engine to have a 6-foot diameter boiler. At 72 tons, No 1000 was also Britain's heaviest eight-wheeled steam locomotive. There was no doubt that Nigel Gresley had created a masterpiece in his o/c 2-6-0, and, classifying it 'H4', the GNR went on to build nine more. The following year the 'H4s' achieved fresh fame, amidst a Miners' Strike and general trade slump, by hauling tremendous trains, sometimes up to 20 coaches, regularly between London and Doncaster. After the Grouping 183 more were built, and the 'K3s',

as the type was now known, became a veritable LNER mainstay with their proven ability to handle any class of traffic. Still producing the clanking noise which hallmarked the RAGTIMERS (qv), the sole defect of the 'K3' was its propensity to 'jump about a bit'. It was this unsteady riding at speed which earned the locos the nickname JAZZERS, after the dance craze of the period. All were withdrawn between 1959 and 1962, and, regrettably, none has been preserved.

JEANIE SHAW

See SCHARNHORST and GNEISENAU.

JENNY LINDS

The talents of Johanna Maria Lind, the legendary Swedish actress and soprano, made an enormous impact on London audiences when she first appeared there in 1847. As a consequence, for years to come many single-wheeled locomotives, all the rage for express work at the time, were nicknamed after her. The sobriquet, above all, implied elegance. The most famous JENNY LINDS were 2-2-2s

GNR 2-6-0 No 1003, seen here hustling a substantial main-line express through Southgate in typical JAZZER style, was, with nine sister engines, the precursor of an important, and numerous, LNER class, the 'K3s'. Built in 1920, No 1003 saw many a change ere it was withdrawn from service, as BR No 61803, in July 1961. *Author's Collection*

of consistently beautiful design which were produced by Sharp Bros, and Craven employed a very similar design on the LB&SCR in 1853-54, at a cost of £2,400 each. Largely due to steaming difficulties, however, the life of the class was not long, and all vanished by 1877. The JENNY LINDS rode beautifully, but they were not large engines.

Derby Works produced its own version for the MR as far back as 1848, forming the genesis of Kirtley's famous 'Singles'.

JENNY RED LEGS
The firm of E.B. Wilson & Co of Leeds, formerly Shepherd & Todd, was also deeply involved in the evolution of the JENNY LIND type. Their locomotive products were invariably highly finished, with mahogany strips, polished and varnished, round the boiler. Two such beauties, o/c 2-2-2s with six-wheeled tenders, of a type styled JENNY

RED LEGS, were supplied by Wilson to the Eastern Counties Railway in May 1847. The engines were renumbered into passenger stock in 1854, but their career as such was short for in 1855 they were rebuilt as 2-4-0STs. They spent the last 15 years of their lives piloting at Bishopsgate Goods Depot, before being scrapped in 1870-71.

JERSEY LILIES
Because of her beauty and charm, Lillie Langtry, the famous Victorian actress and daughter of the Dean of Jersey, was known as the 'Jersey Lily'. So, too, reputedly, were J.G. Robinson's handsome Class '8B' 'Atlantics', 27 of which were built for the GCR in 1903-06. Realising their publicity value, Sir Sam Fay, the General Manager of the GCR, saw to it that the JERSEY LILIES, manned by his Company's best locomen, travelled as far and wide as possible. Thus for over 30 years these locos dominated top main-line work on the

GCR, and only in 1936 were they supplanted by LNER Class 'B7' 4-6-0s. Twenty of the 'Alantics', classified 'C4' by the LNER, survived to enter BR stock, and the last six were scrapped in 1950. Fitted with a Robinson chimney and decked elegantly in green, a JERSEY LILY was certainly a sight never to be forgotten.

It should be added that in recent years O.S. Nock, the well-known railway author, has refuted the theory that the GCR 'Atlantics' were associated in any way with Lillie Langtry, the actress. He firmly maintains that the locomotives earned their nickname because their sheer size and boiler girth reminded some Gorton Works wag of a 32-stone lady, also known as 'Jersey Lillie', who appeared on exhibition at a local pub.

JINTIES
To handle increasing industrial and brewery work, S.W. Johnson designed the MR's first saddle tanks in 1883. By 1897 18 of these diminutive 0-4-0STs had been built, and on account of their 'J' boilers they were known as JINTIES.

The nickname next attached itself, certainly in post-Grouping years, to MR 0-6-0Ts, and from these was evolved the standard LMSR 0-6-0T, of which 415 were built over the years 1924-31, becoming a popular and versatile acquisition throughout the system. No fewer than 10 have been preserved in the UK, and four of these can be found, appropriately enough, at the Midland Railway Centre, Butterley. Locomen on the LMSR Midland Section often referred to the standard 0-6-0Ts as JOCKOS.

JOCKOS
See JINTIES.

JOHNNY DUGANS
See BILL BAILEYS.

Caught shunting at Derby in August 1935, ex-MR JINTY No 1509 was built there, out of Revenue account, as No 1117A in 1893. Rebuilt in 1915, the little 0-4-0ST retained its second MR number, 1509, when it was taken into LMSR stock. *Author*

JONES BOGIES

In 1873 David Jones introduced the HR's first 4-4-0s when he rebuilt two Hawthorn 2-4-0s. He then consolidated the issue by designing his 'Duke' Class 4-4-0s, 10 of which were built for the HR by Dubs & Co in 1874. Massive, powerful engines for their time, the 'Dukes', known colloquially as the JONES BOGIES and named to a man, introduced several new features which were a significant hallmark of things to come. All survived to enter LMSR stock, but the class had disappeared by 1930. See also LOCHGORM BOGIES.

JONES GOODS

The first 4-6-0s to appear on any British railway (though the NER never conceded the fact!), 15 of these locomotives were delivered to the HR by Sharp Stewart & Co in 1894. Arriving too late for the current tourist season, they were thoroughly at home by the time the 1895 season commenced, and were triumphantly successful in handling both passenger and goods trains. Designed by David Jones, hence their nickname, the locos were radical in appearance as well as design. Outside cylinders were *not* embodied in the frame, as had been HR practice for decades, and spark arresters were fitted into the base of their distinctive louvred chimneys. No 103, withdrawn by the LMSR in 1934, was later stored at St Rollox Works, then, repainted in Stroudley yellow livery, it was restored to traffic in 1959. In 1966 it was found a permanent home at the Glasgow Museum of Transport. These pioneer 4-6-0s were first popularly known as the LARGE GOODS.

JUBILEE JUMPERS

J. Holden's first design for the GER, reflecting as acute shortage of shunting tanks on that railway, produced a total of 50 Class 'T18' 0-6-0Ts. It was soon found, however, that these little tanks could also handle suburban passenger traffic much better than the four-coupled types which were presently being employed. Thus a long line of BUCK JUMPERS (qv) was established once the last 10 'T18s', built in 1888, were fitted with the Westinghouse brake. The fact that 20 of the class were built in 1887, the year of Queen Victoria's Golden Jubilee, was sufficient excuse to attach the nickname JUBILEE JUMPERS to the whole class. Later classified 'J66' by the LNER, 19 of them survived to enter BR stock in 1948, plus, of course, one recovered from the Mersey Electric Railway, and placed in Service Stock. The last 'J66' in running stock, No 68383, was withdrawn from Staveley in October 1955.

JUBILEE PUGS

These engines were so named because the first 10 were also built in 1887, at St Rollox Works. Fairly substantial 0-6-0STs, they were designed by Dugald Drummond for work around the various docklands which were operated by the CR. Each loco weighed 43¾ tons, as opposed to the 31 tons of the smaller DOCK PUGS (qv) which Drummond introduced one year later. By 1890 20 more JUBILEE PUGS were added. Most acquired LMSR numbers in due course, but the class had disappeared by 1930.

JUBILEES

This name was first applied to a series of splendid 0-4-2 tender engines which were designed by William Adams for the LSWR. The first 10 were shopped from Nine Elms Works once again in 1887, the 50th year of Queen Victoria's reign. Nine Elms built 40 more by 1895, and Neilson & Co provided 40 in 1892-95; it was the locomotives' immediate success which induced Adams, at a time when Nine Elms Works was fully occupied, to order the latter engines. Very much 'maids of all work', the JUBILEES handled all classes of LSWR work with ease. When, in 1892, the LSWR Directors inquired why double-heading seemed necessary for West of England fast goods trains, Adams had his reply ready. The use of JUBILEES, he informed them, had so improved timekeeping in that area that tonnage had increased by 20 per cent. Ergo, longer trains were justified, with occasional assistance from pilot engines! When Queen Victoria died at Osborne in 1901 it was a JUBILEE which was specially

The last LSWR JUBILEE to be built by Neilson & Co (Works No 4545/1893), No 646 and her sisters differed in detail from the Nine Elms series, but only weighed 2 cwt more. No 646, withdrawn in May 1939, finished her days at Salisbury shed, supplying steam to Bulleid's new 'Merchant Navy' 'Pacifics' as they stood at the running shed between trains. Eventually the JUBILEE was cut up in 1944. *Author's Collection*

ANTELOPE (qv) No 61008 *Kudu* (left) vies with JUBILEE No 45694 *Bellerophon* for attention at Neasden shed on 3 June 1962. *Author*

prepared to haul her funeral train from Gosport to Fareham. Ninety of the class entered SR stock, and although withdrawals commenced seriously in the 1930s, the last, ex-No 612, survived to 1951. It must be admitted, though, that, as DS 3191, she supplied steam to Eastleigh Boiler Yard for the last four years of her life. See also EMERALD QUEEN.

Also popularly known as JUBILEES, though neither designed nor built during either of Queen Victoria's Jubilee years, were 50 GER '1090' Class 2-4-2Ts built at Stratford in 1893-1902, again to J. Holden's design. A tank version of the INTERMEDIATE (qv) 2-4-0s, these sturdy engines were purpose-built for the GER's outer suburban services, which were then expanding to Southend and Southminster. Most substantial of all the GER 2-4-2Ts, they were classified 'F3' by the LNER, and although a dozen were withdrawn in the late 1930s, ten more years elapsed before more were scrapped. The last, BR No 67127, was not taken out of service until April 1953.

The LMSR's JUBILEES were introduced in 1934, the year which marked the 25th anniversary of King George V's reign, and all were named in due course in appropriate Empire and Naval terms. These o/c 4-6-0s, 191 of which were built by December 1936, were an improved version of the LMSR BABY SCOT (qv), had coned boilers and top feed, and fitted easily into the new LMSR standardisation programme which W.A. Stanier was rapidly implementing. Though used extensively on main-line duties, the JUBILEES somehow never quite earned the encomiums which were being heaped on the BLACK FIVES (qv). Nevertheless, the ability of the JUBILEES to work on the Midland Section of the LMSR, where larger engines were barred, made them extremely useful locomotives. Two were rebuilt in 1942, to emerge almost indistinguishable from Stanier-built 'Royal Scots'. All, of course, passed into BR hands, and, apart from *Windward Islands*, a sad casualty of the Harrow disaster of 8 October 1952, withdrawal on a general scale did not commence until

1960-61. Four of the last survivors, withdrawn in 1966-67, have been preserved. The LMSR JUBILEES were also known to some as RED STANIERS.

JUMBOS
This is probably the most popular locomotive nickname. 'Jumbo' was a famous circus elephant which met its death in America in 1852, and the word became synonymous with 'elephant' in public usage, and was usually employed to denote good-natured, if rather lumbering, strength.

From 1859, for decades to come, the LNWR came to rely heavily on tough little 2-2-2s and 2-4-0s in handling much of its express work on the West Coast line. The 2-2-2s, known officially as the 'Lady of the Lake' and 'Problem' Classes, thoroughly earned their nickname JUMBOS as they wrestled with heavy trains. Built by Ramsbottom in 1859-61, the single-wheelers, with 7 ft 6 in driving wheels, were still working lighter trains, and acting as pilots, at the turn of the century; the last did not vanish until 1907, while two, *Marmion* and *Waverley*, performed nobly in the Railway Races of 1888.

Then Webb introduced his famous 2-4-0s, with smaller coupled wheels, in 1874. They became immediate favourites with LNWR men, and were soon dubbed LITTLE JUMBOS. The exploits of *Charles Dickens* and *Hardwicke*, to name only two, are legendary; happily, the latter remains with us to this day. Many did not survive to acquire LMS numbers, but the last in service, No 25001 *Snowdon*, did not bow the knee until October 1934. The only fault of these great little engines was their size—they had to be flogged with anything above an average load, whence they became extravagant consumers of coal.

William Stroudley, in replacing elderly LB&SCR Craven 0-6-0s, introduced two powerful Class 'C' 0-6-0s of his own design in 1871. Kitson & Co provided 12 more in 1873-74, and Brighton Works added a further six in 1873. Reception of the Class 'Cs' by locomen was mixed; some found them acceptable, others criticised them as poor steamers, sluggish in performance, and heavy on coal and water. They tended, too, to roll on weak sections of track, All in all, they soon merited the nickname JUMBOS. All accumulated respectable mileages, however, before the last, No 420, was withdrawn in December 1904, having run 622,153 miles in all.

The next JUMBOS were W.G. Beattie's 4-4-0s of 1876-77, built in Glasgow for the LSWR (see BEATTIE'S FOLLY). All 20 proved to be bad steamers, and were a direct cause of Beattie's retirement in 1879 on grounds of 'ill health'. Beattie, living on at Surbiton to 1918, contrived, nevertheless, to outlive his two successors! William Adams rebuilt the JUMBOS, but nearly all were scrapped by 1894. Basically they were over-cylindered; their frames cracked easily, and the design of their piston valves was also suspect.

Equally disastrous was the purchase by the Swindon, Marlborough & Andover Railway in 1882 of an Avonside-built 0-4-4 Fairlie double-bogied tank. Numbered 4, and nick-named JUMBO because of its failure as a passenger engine, it was kept very much in reserve, and was scrapped under M&SWJR auspices in 1892, although the boiler was retained for use at the Company's workshops in Cirencester. Ironically, it was one of the first locomotives in Britain to employ the Walschaerts valve gear.

Conversely, James Stirling's famous SER Class 'F' 4-4-0s, also known to locomen as JUMBOS, were immensely popular with a railway-minded public, and 88 were built at Ashford Works between 1883 and 1898, proving to be thoroughly reliable and speedy engines. No 240, named *Onward* to attend the Paris Exhibition of 1889, won a Gold Medal there, albeit her name was removed immediately she returned to the UK. French railway authorities were very impressed by

Shopped from Ashford in May 1893 at a remarkably low cost of £1,795, ex-SER JUMBO No A172 was one of 12 Class 'Fs' which were never rebuilt to 'F1' specification. Withdrawn in 1930, A172 spent some months outside Ramsgate shed, before being towed away, in December 1930, to Ashford Works for breaking up. Final mileage was 1,042,197. *Author's Collection*

the British exhibits, and trials arranged in France between *Onward* and LB&SCR 0-4-2 *Edward Blount* were those during which William Stroudley contracted his fatal chill. Most SE&CR JUMBOS were rebuilt latterly to Class 'F1', and as such nine entered BR stock. The last, No 1231, was withdrawn in March 1949.

The smallest JUMBOS of all were 0-4-0 tanks and saddle tanks which were supplied by Neilson & Co of Glasgow to the Gas, Light & Coke Co Ltd over the years 1878-1900; over 40 miles of standard gauge track were in use at the latter's Beckton plant. The saddle tanks had specially cut-down fittings to enable them to enter gas retorts, and No 25 of the species (Works No 5087/1896) can still be seen at Bressingham Steam Museum.

The largest, and heaviest, JUMBOS, weighing 92¾ tons, were five massive 4-6-4Ts which were designed for the FR by D.L.Rutherford, and built by Kitson & Co in 1920-21. Forbidden to work north of Barrow because of their weight, these JUMBOS were classified '3P' by the LMSR. They did not last long, however, in new colours: four were withdrawn in the mid-1930s, and the last, No 11103, went in 1940.

Another, rather nondescript, JUMBO put in a UK appearance in 1883, when the 5,000th locomotive constructed by the Baldwin Locomotive Co of Philadelphia Works, USA, was shipped to England in parts, to be put together again at the L&YR's Horwich Works. The object of the exercise was to demonstrate the efficacy of the Eames Vacuum Brake System. The reconstructed engine, a 4-2-2 named *Lovett Eames*, made several trips on L&YR and GNR metals, and for more than a year it was stabled at the GNR's Wood Green depot. There, because of the locomotive's 'buzzer', or foghorn whistle, it was known to local inhabitants as JUMBO. Her bell, engraved with the name *Lovett Eames*, hung at King's Cross shed for many years.

A further recipient of the nickname JUMBO was an early 0-6-0 goods engine design by Dugald Drummond for the CR. Based substantially on his earlier NBR type,

the first-built came from Neilson & Co in 1883. These 0-6-0s proved to be much more powerful than anything that had gone before. Ultimately, perpetuated by H. Smellie, J. Lambie and J.F. McIntosh, the class was increased to 244 engines; held in great affection by CR men, they rapidly mastered all types of traffic. Many were fitted with the Westinghouse brake to work passenger trains. Remarkably, all passed into LMSR ownership, whence they were subjected to little alteration, though quite a number acquired stovepipe chimneys. More remarkably still, nearly all survived to have 40000 added to their numbers by BR, and the last was not withdrawn until 1962.

In some areas, any MR locomotive was often referred to as a JUMBO.

For one final class of JUMBO, see SQUARE CABS.

JUMBO THE SECOND

Robert Urie's first design for the LSWR, part of his 'big engine' policy, materialised in 1914 in the form of 10 robustly constructed two-cylindered MT 4-6-0s, known as the 'H15' Class. They proved an excellent investment at £3,950 apiece, and it was probably their sheer size which prompted the driver of any one of them to refer to his charge as JUMBO THE SECOND. Ten more were added by the SR in 1924, at a rather alarming price of £10,308 each. Drummond's Class 'E14' No 335 had already been rebuilt to the 'H15' Class in 1914, and his five 'F13' 4-6-0s, practically unemployed by the time Grouping arrived, were dealt with similarly in 1924. Thus the 'H15' Class eventually numbered 26. All lasted well into the 1950s, and the last four were not withdrawn until December 1961.

JUMBO THE SECOND. The massive smokebox of ex-LSWR Class 'H15' No 487 shows to advantage in this Eastleigh study, taken in SR days. Rebuilt with a Maunsell superheater in 1929, and later renumbered 30487 by BR, the engine was a comparatively early withdrawal in November 1957. *Steamchest*

KILLIN TANKS

When, in 1885, St Rollox Works produced eight little CR 0-4-0STs at a cost of £700 each, Dugald Drummond authorised construction of two more—this time in the form of 0-4-2STs. These were sent to work on the Killin Railway when the latter opened on 13 March 1896. To enable them to handle passenger trains on this steeply-graded line, both 'pugs' were fitted with the Westinghouse brake. Later the coal capacity of their bunkers was stepped up to 1¼ tons. The first of the so-called KILLIN TANKS never lived to carry its allotted LMSR number, but sister engine No 15001 worked on until April 1947.

THE KING'S ENGINE

This was a somewhat notorious 'long boiler' six-wheeler which was presented, it is said, to the Eastern Counties Railway by its Chairman, George Hudson, widely known as the 'Railway King'. The MR had acquired the engine when it was built by Rothwell & Co in 1846, and Kitson & Co duly supplied a six-wheeled tender. The six-wheeler's life on the ECR seems, however, to have been both brief and unfortunate; it was sold on to a Mr Richardson in 1857.

KLONDYKES

When H.A. Ivatt shopped the GNR's, and Britain's, first 'Atlantic' in 1898, the Western world was gripped by Gold Rush fever—and KLONDYKES the type became. No 990 remained the sole example for two years, then 10 more were added in 1900, and the class was doubled by 1903. Though destined to be overshadowed by the larger 'Atlantic' which Ivatt introduced in 1902, the initial emergence of the KLONDYKE made an emormous impression on all concerned. Even the fact that No 990 was too long for the

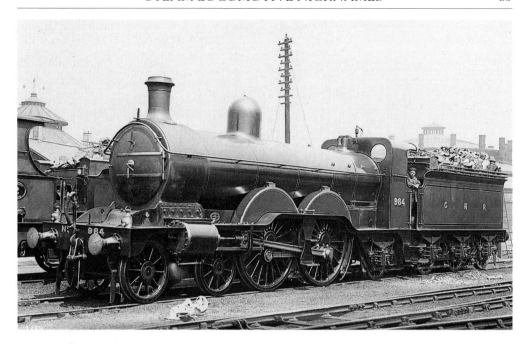

The beauty of the GNR's KLONDYKE No 984 speaks for itself in this Peterborough study. One of 10 added by Doncaster (Works No 876) in 1900, this engine was superheated by the LNER in May 1924, and was withdrawn, as No 3984, in October 1937. *Author's Collection*

King's Cross turntable, and had to move out to Hornsey to be turned, was regarded with awe, rather than in realistic terms. The LNER classified the type 'C2', and withdrawals did not begin until 1935. None lived to enter BR stock, but the prototype, No 990 *Henry Oakley*, was retained for preservation, and can now be seen at the National Railway Museum, York.

A group of 20 Class 'F20' 0-6-0Ts, shopped by the L&YR in 1897, also fell heir to the KLONDYKE nickname. Five survived to enter BR stock, and the last, No 51544, worked on until June 1959.

KNICK KNACKS

A final development of Ivatt's 0-6-0 design for the GNR. The first 15 were built in 1911, and with almost yearly additions right up to 1922, both the LNER and BR inherited 110 of this extremely useful 'J6' Class. They worked express goods until the Gresley 2-6-0s arrived on the scene, and were great favourites with GNR men, who often referred

to them as 'A' engines because of their original GNR classification. To many, however, these locomotives were better known as KNICK KNACKS, an affectionate reference to the odd noise they made when running with steam shut off. Although withdrawals commenced in 1955, the majority lingered on until 1958. By June 1962, however, all had gone.

KRUGERS

Remarkable and impressive looking outside-framed locomotives, these were designed by William Dean for the GWR. No 2601 came first, in December 1899: a 4-6-0 with a massive Belpaire firebox and the largest grate area in Britain. Events in South Africa that year, plus the engine's formidable and belligerent appearance, earned it the nickname KRUGER. A second engine followed in 1901, but this time the 2-6-0 wheel arrangement was employed, and that design was adhered to when eight more followed in 1903. The boiler was daringly advanced in

When No 2601, the GWR's only 4-6-0 KRUGER, was built at Swindon in 1899 it carried a boiler pressure of 200 lbs. This was soon reduced to 180 lbs, and some of the subsequent 2-6-0 KRUGERS were shopped with pressure further reduced to 165 lbs. The whole class, however, had short lives, and No 2601, withdrawn in December 1904, ran only 67,000 miles. *Steamchest*

conception, and, inevitably, trouble was experienced. The question of rebuilding all 10 locomotives was considered, but in the light of the immediate success of the much more compact ABERDARES (qv) the idea was abandoned. The KRUGERS consequently led very short lives, and all had perished by January 1907.

L

LADY MARY
See MARYS.

LANKY TANKS
A sobriquet which embraced all tank engines built by the L&YR, and one used most affectionately with reference to the ever-popular Horwich-built 2-4-2Ts. Tank engines on the L&YR were also known as PUGS (qv).

LARGE Bs
Based to some degree on a Kirtley design, this robust type of 0-6-0 was introduced on the SE&CR by H. Wainwright in 1900; 79 were built at Ashford, and 30 more were provided by outside firms. Although classified 'C' by Ashford, these engines were referred to as 'B3s' in the Longhedge Locomotive Register, and many old Chatham drivers insisted on speaking of them as LARGE Bs. Many were reboilered, but, that apart, little change other than reduction in chimney height was effected. All entered SR stock in 1923, and all but two lived to be handed on to BR. The class totalled 109 at its peak, and the last, No DS239, was withdrawn in May 1967. Fortunately it can still be seen, as SE&CR No 592, on the Bluebell Railway.

LARGE BLOOMERS
See BLOOMERS.

LARGE BOGIES
See SMALL BOGIES.

LARGE DREADNOUGHTS
See DREADNOUGHTS.

LARGE GOODS
See JONES GOODS.

LARGE HAWTHORNS
See SMALL HAWTHORNS.

LARGE HOPPERS
See GRASSHOPPERS.

LARGE SCOTCHMEN
A group of six Class 'D' 0-4-2WTs which were supplied to the LC&DR by Neilson & Co of Glasgow in 1873. With inside frames, except for radial wheels, they still weighed only 5 cwt more than the earlier vintage SCOTCHMEN (qv), a product of the same firm. Again, provision of romantic Scottish names reinforced their nickname. The last, No 100, was withdrawn in December 1913.

THE LAWNMOWER
Despite Colonel Stephens's fondness for emplying second-hand steam locomotives throughout his light railway 'empire', he had the foresight to recognise that the introduction of internal combustion units might conceivably be the salvation of many a light railway. One such was the tiny petrol-engined loco which was supplied to the 3-foot gauge Rye & Camber Tramway by the Kent Construction Co of Ashford in 1925. Strictly outside the range of this book, and hardly prepossessing in appearance, the little machine none the less served local needs until the light railway closed in 1939. At least one Rye & Camber devotee has described the loco's nickname THE LAWNMOWER as

LARGE SCOTCHMAN No 96 *Thanet*, later SE&CR No 554, was built by Neilson & Co (Works No 1742) in February 1873. The locomotive spent its last four years on shunting and empty stock duties, and its cumulative mileage of 833,641, when withdrawn in June 1910, was the lowest of the class. *Author's Collection*

'vulgar'. One would have thought that anyone with a sense of humour witnessing the small tractor in action could hardly fail to share the joke.

LIGHTNING

The nickname given to the GWR's first home-built locomotive while it was under construction at Swindon in 1846. Turned out in 13 weeks, the engine was formally christened *Great Western* when it entered service. Built as a 2-2-2 to demonstrate broad gauge potentialities, it was later rebuilt as a 4-2-2, and as such completed 370,687 miles before all broad gauge locomotives were withdrawn in 1892.

LILLIPUTIAN

This nickname was applied to the earliest known British example of a 'light locomotive', ie one which could carry a few passengers in its own right. The machine, a four-wheeled carriage with vertical boiler forward, and seating for seven passengers in the rear, was designed by the Eastern Counties Railway's Engineer, James Samuel, and was delivered by Fairfield Works, Bow, in April 1847. Named *Express*, it was often referred to as the LILLIPUTIAN. On 23 December what was described as 'a successful run' was made between London and Cambridge, with several Press representatives on board. During six months of 1848 the little locomotive ran 5,526 miles with an average coke consumption of 3.02 lbs per mile. Its main function, though, lay in carrying engineers and staff about on inspection duties.

LITTLE DICK

When GCR 0-6-0ST No 889, built in 1897, was converted a few years later to an 0-6-2ST, and fitted with a 4-ton crane, it was assigned to Gorton Works for yard shunting. There it became known as LITTLE DICK. Then, in 1918, the crane was removed, and the engine was restored to normal condition. It was the only crane loco the GCR ever possessed. Three of the 0-6-0STs, Class 'J62' in LNER stock, lasted to BR days, and LITTLE DICK had only just perished in December 1947.

LITTLE EGBERTS

To meet demands for heavy banking and coal shunting around the Accrington area, the L&YR constructed four large 0-8-2Ts in 1908. The working weight of these giants was 84 tons, and they were soon nicknamed LITTLE EGBERTS—after a well-known troupe of performing elephants! Unsuperheated, they owned the largest boilers then built at Horwich, and the 21½-inch diameter of their (inside) cylinders was greater than any other simple expansion locomotive in the UK. The inner pair of driving wheels were left flangeless to assist in negotiating curves, and oval-shaped buffers were fitted. Eventually, being a small non-standard class, the LITTLE EGBERTS met a predictably speedy fate at LMSR hands; the last, L&YR No 1504, never destined to bear its allotted LMSR number, 11803, slipped away in October 1929.

LITTLE JENNY

Not long after taking over the management of the NLR on 1 January 1909, the LNWR, in its search for economies, displaced NLR Adams 4-4-0Ts (see BROAD STREET RATTLERS) from Acton–Hammersmith branch work by introducing a one-class 48-seater steam railmotor designed by George Whale. Soon nicknamed LITTLE JENNY by locals, the railcar offered a half-hourly weekday service from 4 January 1909; several additional timber halts were opened to encourage branch traffic, and local tickets were issued on board by conductor guards. Alas, success was short-lived: LITTLE JENNY was replaced by an LNWR petrol-electric railmotor on 9 March 1913, and passenger working on the branch ultimately ceased on 31 December 1916. LITTLE JENNY, one of eight which had been built in 1905-10, duly passed into LMSR ownership, and the last of these steam units perished in 1948.

THE LITTLE KINETON

This was a contractor's 0-6-0ST which was first hired, then later purchased, by the East & West Junction Railway when passenger services were inaugurated between Kineton

The LITTLE EGBERTS' 4 ft 6 in driving wheels added punch to the engines' capacity for banking heavy coal trains in the Accrington area. No 1505, the last-built of the four in April 1908, was allotted LMSR No 11804, but perished, still carrying its L&YR number, in February 1927. *Author's Collection*

THE LITTLE KINETON. A fascinating example of Colonel Stephens's opportunism, No 4 *Morous*, having survived sundry owners, was still handling the 10.35 am Selsey Tramway goods in the late 1920s. *Author's Collection*

and Fenny Compton in 1871. Used latterly in Woodford gravel pits, the saddle tank, rebuilt in 1910, was sold to the Shropshire & Montgomeryshire Light Railway, where, at Colonel Stephens's behest, it became No 4 *Morous*. In 1924, still retaining its name and number, it moved on to the Selsey Tramway, and served thereon until it was scrapped in 1936.

LITTLE MAILS
See MAILS.

LITTLE SHARPS
The Manchester firm of Sharp Roberts & Co, later known as Sharp Stewart & Co Ltd, of Atlas Works, Glasgow, built its first locomotive in 1833, and delivered three engines to the London & Brighton Railway in 1839. All were 2-2-2s, and had cylinders 14 in x 18 in, in contrast to four 13 in x 18 in 'singles' which were built for the London & Croydon Railway at about the same time. The boiler barrels were 8 feet long, and the type came to be known as the EARLY SHARPS. Five years later, Sharp supplied the London & Brighton with six more 2-2-2s, this time with 15 in x 20 in cylinders and 10-foot boiler barrels. These were known as LITTLE, or ENLARGED, SHARPS. They met with a lot of teething trouble, and were ultimately rebuilt at their makers' expense. Yet, when the Brighton Directors conducted a survey in 1846 to ascertain which manufacturer supplied the best express passenger design, Sharp engines came top of the list, and drivers showed a distinct preference for them.

On the SER, meanwhile, Cudworth produced six new 2-4-0s in 1858-59, using many parts salvaged from earlier Sharp singles. They were attractive little secondary passenger engines, double-framed and fitted with coal-burning fireboxes. Because of their origins, however, they readily became known as LITTLE SHARPS. Later condemned by James Stirling, all went by November 1881.

LITTLE SHARPIES
Here we have a mildly colloquial version of the same theme. When the GNR was formed

in 1847 its first engines were 50 Sharp 'singles'. With 5 ft 6 in driving wheels and forward domes, the locomotives weighed nearly 18½ tons. Archibald Sturrock later converted 31 of them into 2-2-2Ts, but rather spoiled the trim appearance of the LITTLE SHARPIES by adding 3 feet to the wheelbase. Although these conversions served the GNR well, they oscillated at the rear end when running at speed, and footplatemen soon dubbed them TAILWAGGERS. Later still, in 1871-73, four LITTLE SHARPIES which had been further converted into 0-4-2Ts were thoroughly rebuilt by Patrick Stirling as 0-4-2 well tanks. One of these, No 43, saw the end of the LITTLE SHARPIES era in October 1896.

More from the same stable came the GER's way, when S.W. Johnson introduced his well-known, and long-lived, class of 2-4-0 light passenger engine. Ten were built at Stratford, and 30 more were added by Sharp Stewart in 1867-71. Beautifully designed, the latter were affectionately known to GER men as LITTLE SHARPIES. James Holden rebuilt the whole series in 1889-91 with longer cabs and larger driving wheels, thus adding to the overall weight. But even as scrapping of the class commenced in 1901, 14 LITTLE SHARPIES were rebuilt with increased boiler pressure. As it happened, No 1, the first to be built, was the last to be scrapped, in December 1913.

LITTLE TICH
This was an LB&SCR TERRIER (qv) 0-6-0T which was acquired by the SE&CR in September 1904 to work the Sheppey Light Railway's goods services. The little locomotive became a firm favourite on the Island, and was nicknamed LITTLE TICH, after Harry Relph, then all the rage in London music halls as 'The Man of Kent'. After her boiler was condemned in 1909, LITTLE TICH never returned to Sheppey, despite several urgent appeals by Sheerness shed staff. A very widely travelled locomotive in her day, she was renumbered 680S in SR Departmental Stock in 1932, whereafter she settled down as the Lancing Carriage Works

LITTLE SHARPIE No 160 is seen here as supplied new by Sharp Stewart & Co (Works No 2114) to the GER in March 1871. Subsequently rebuilt at Stratford in 1892, the locomotive was Duplicate Listed as 0160 in 1901, and was broken up one year later. *Author's Collection*

shunter. Withdrawn by BR as DS680 in June 1962, LITTLE TICH was spared, to be restored to LB&SCR livery, whence she was despatched, once again as No 54 *Waddon*, to Canada for preservation.

LIVELY POLLY

This nickname was bestowed on the Liverpool Overhead Railway's solitary steam locomotive. An 0-4-0WT, built by Kitson & Co in 1893, it served the LOR's engineering department on odd jobs for 55 years. Length over buffers of the little i/c tank was only 12 feet, and the engine weighed 10 tons 2 cwt in working order. Sold in 1948, it was overhauled at Rea Ltd's coal wharf at Birkenhead. An engine very similar to LIVELY POLLY was supplied to the Corringham Light Railway, also in 1893.

LOBSTERS

Presumably in amused analogy to the LMSR CRAB (qv) 2-6-0s, W.A. Stanier's new 'Moguls', 40 of which were introduced in 1933, were referred to by some as LOBSTERS. Despite that, they were much more conventional in appearance than subsequent 2-6-0 types which were built by the LMSR. See also CAMELS.

LOCHGORM BOGIES

Moving boldly to meet increased traffic requirements on the HR, David Jones had 10 'Duke' Class 4-4-0s built by Dubs & Co (Works Nos 714-23) during the latter half of 1874. Later, subject only to minor modifications to boiler and tender, the HR's own Works at Lochgorm turned out seven more. Their construction was spread over the years 1876-88 and, for obvious reasons, these last seven became known to HR men as the LOCHGORM BOGIES. The last of the Dubs contingent went in August 1923, together with the last four BOGIES. See also JONES BOGIES.

LONGBACKS

The first LONGBACKS were two engines

Already 60 years old, the little 0-4-0WT which was known on the Liverpool Overhead Railway as LIVELY POLLY was captured by the camera at Birkenhead on 29 August 1955. *LCGB/Ken Nunn Collection*

which were bought by the Londonderry & Enniskillen Railway from John Jones of Liverpool in 1855. The locomotives were too long for the Company's 15-foot turntables, and also occasioned complaints of excessive coke consumption. Latterly the builders agreed to knock £100 off the original purchase price. The LONGBACKS lasted 18 years under GNR (Ireland) auspices, and were withdrawn in 1876.

A series of eight 5-foot 0-6-0s, built by the NBR at St Margarets Works in 1868-69, were similarly nicknamed because of the inordinate length of their domeless boilers. Double-framed, these sturdy old engines underwent a rebuild by Matthew Holmes between 1888 and 1898, and all were withdrawn during the years 1912-14.

LONG STOMACHS
See SHOOTING GALLERIES.

LONG TOMS
These were the GNR's first 0-8-0 tender engines; designed by H.A. Ivatt, they were regarded at the time as being of notable size and power. Their unusually long boilers, likened by many to the long-barrelled naval guns which were fashionable at that period, earned them their nickname. Fifty-five were built between 1901 and 1909, and in their early days they looked doubly impressive painted green. One, No 417, was chosen, together with small 'Atlantic' No 988, to undergo initial trials on the GNR with the Schmidt superheater. The last five LONG TOMS were so equipped when built, and a majority of the others received superheaters in later years.

Extremely powerful engines, the LONG TOMS, soon also nicknamed BRICK ENGINES, dominated heavy freight and mineral traffic between Peterborough and London until after the First World War, when sufficient 2-8-0s became available for the purpose. The appetite of the LONG TOMS for coal, however, was so voracious that firemen had to be paid an extra 3d a day for working them. The last survivor, No 3420, by then LNER Class 'Q3', was withdrawn from the West Riding in February 1937. See also SEA PIGS.

LONG TOM TANKS

Another bold step by Ivatt saw an 0-8-2T version of the Long Toms introduced in 1903. The total weight of this new monster was 79 tons; this so alarmed the Metropolitan Railway that it insisted on having the locomotive rebuilt to lighter dimensions before it would allow it to work on the GNR's Moorgate section. Forty more of these LONG TOM TANKS, as they soon became known, were built at Doncaster in 1904-06. Difficulty in running through some Metropolitan tunnels was, however, still being experienced, and within four years all 41 tanks were sent to fresh pastures in the West Riding and Nottingham. Though a few returned to London at the end of hostilities, and were employed

on carriage shunting at King's Cross, the late 1920s saw the onset of withdrawals, and by February 1934 all had gone. At Colwick depot they were known to LNER men as 'Baltics'. The name is technically incorrect, of course, but no doubt the impressive size of these tanks inspired its use. LNER classification was 'R1'.

LORD NELSON

This somewhat inconsequential nickname was conferred upon LSWR Class 'M7' 0-4-0T No 111 when the locomotive was stationed at Strawberry Hill shed during the 1920s. One of the last 'M7s' to go, No 30111 was withdrawn in January 1964.

LUFTWAFFE TANKS

Three classes of Metropolitan Railway locomotives taken over by the LNER on 1 November 1937 included eight very handsome 4-4-4Ts. Designed by Charles Jones,

The first (Works No 1119) of a final batch of 20 LONG TOM TANKS which were subscribed by Doncaster in 1906, No 3137 spent its last two years shunting carriages at Hornsey, before being withdrawn in August 1931. Some months later came an LNER proposal to alter surviving 'R1s' to diesel-engined compressed air operation. The industrial depression of the 1930s put paid to the scheme, however. *Author's Collection*

and supplied to the Met in 1920-21 by Kerr Stuart & Co for fast passenger work, all remained at the LNER's Neasden shed until December 1941, whence the whole class was transferred to the Nottingham area. Never highly regarded by the LNER men at Colwick shed, they were dismissed there rather cavalierly as LUFTWAFFE TANKS, ie almost German agents! Despite wartime economies, the first withdrawal was effected in 1942. The last, No 7511, LNER classification 'H2', went in November 1947.

THE LURCHER
The Isle of Wight railway, the Freshwater, Yarmouth & Newport, purchased a 20 hp Drewry petrol railcar in July 1913. It could accommodate 12 passengers, and was usually employed on special duties during the summer months. Sometimes it stood in reserve when one of the FYNR's two steam locomotives required attention. FYNR men knew the Drewry car as THE LURCHER, because it see-sawed so much on the track, whatever speed was being recorded.

M

MAC'S MANGLE
This immortal nickname was lavished on LNWR No 227, a 2-2-2 which was built at Wolverton Works in 1849 to J.E. McConnell's design. Outside cylinders, frames and axle bearings contributed to the locomotive's abnormal width, and some station platforms had to be cut back to accommodate her passage. Her driving wheels were of 6 ft 6 in diameter, and the engine was cut up in 1863.

MAGGIE MURPHIES
When J.G. Robinson introduced his Class '8K' 2-8-0s on the GCR in 1911 no one could have foreseen the impact the type was to make on British railways over the next half-century. By 1912 126 had been built for the GCR, and over 500 more were commissioned by the Government for service abroad during the First World War. Many were subsequently hired, or bought, by British railway companies in post-war years; originally styled the 'MM' Class because their construction had been sponsored by the Ministry of Munitions, the type latterly became known as RODs (qv). The GWR purchased 100 of them, and these were given running numbers 3000-99. Because of their earlier 'MM' classification, GWR men referred to them as MAGGIE MURPHIES. Forty-five of this hardy species survived life on the GWR to enter service with BR in 1948.

MAIDSTONES
James Stirling's maiden design for the SER, his Class 'A' i/c 4-4-0s, were very similar to those he had introduced on the G&SWR a few years earlier, and 12 were built at Ashford Works during 1879-81. Indifferent runners on passenger trains, the whole class was concentrated on Cannon Street–Maidstone services. Nicknamed accordingly MAIDSTONES and DARTFORD BOGIES, the locos duly entered SE&CR stock on 1 January 1899, but within 10 years all except three were relegated to the Duplicate list, and the last of Stirling's Class 'As' perished, all too soon, in June 1909.

MAILS/MAIL SINGLES
James Cudworth was responsible for eight six-wheeled singles being delivered to the SER by Sharp Bros in 1851, at a cost of £1,980 each. Six more were built at Ashford Works in 1856-57; speedy, hardy engines, they were subsequently known as MAILS because of their regular employment on Continental services from Bricklayers Arms. Later, when larger singles took over, Cudworth's earlier engines became a shade less fashionable as LITTLE MAILS, although actually Cudworth was to have the last laugh (see IRON-CLADS). The new replacements, soon known as MAIL SINGLES, had 7-foot driving wheels, and, again designed by Cudworth, the first two were built at Ashford in July 1861. The following year the Vulcan Foundry

MAIL SINGLE No 200 is seen here as supplied to the SER by the Vulcan Foundry in May 1862. In keeping with current practice, sand containers were sited around the dome cover, and the six-wheeled tender carried 3 tons of coal and 2,500 gallons of water. Laid aside at Ashford around September 1887, the locomotive was hired by the Army for work at Dover Harbour a few months before it was finally sold for scrap in September 1888. *Author's Collection*

and Kitson & Co subscribed four more each, and Ashford built a final dozen in 1865-77. No 199 achieved unwonted notoriety by being involved in an accident at Staplehurst on 9 June 1865. Charles Dickens was a passenger that day, and, badly shaken, he never really recovered, dying, in the event, on the fifth anniversary of the accident. The MAIL SINGLES soldiered on, but all were withdrawn by February 1890.

MANSON 4-4-0s
Although James Manson designed five classes of 4-4-0s in all for the G&SWR, it was his very first which persisted in Sou' Western men's minds as the MANSON 4-4-0s. Fifty-seven of these Class '8s' were built at Kilmarnock in 1892-1904, their design based on Manson's earlier experience with the GNSR.

However, handsome engines though they were, they could not match Hugh Smellie's immortal BIG BOGIES (qv) for speed. Fifty-three MANSON 4-4-0s reached the Grouping; then, falling foul of LMS standardisation policy, they vanished by 1933. The last survivor was No 14170.

MARY
The SKYE BOGIES (qv) were very popular with HR men, and, although the locomotives were unnamed, at least five of them were affectionately nicknamed, all using the suffix 'Mary'. These were No 70 QUEEN MARY, No 85 LADY MARY, No 87 PRINCESS MARY, No 6 (33) FIERY MARY, and No 48 ENCHANTING MARY. Withdrawal of the class started with LADY MARY in August 1923, and ended with QUEEN MARY, by

then LMSR No 14277, in June 1930.

MATCHBOXES

The GWR's devotion to six-coupled pannier tanks flowered from 1929 onwards with the production of several hundred '5700' Class engines. Universally popular as well throughout BR's Western Region, the locomotives' cheerful nickname, MATCHBOXES, was, no doubt, as much a reflection on their four-square appearance as anything else. Quite a number still work for a living on various preserved lines.

MELDRUM MEG

William Cowan, appointed Locomotive Superintendent to the GNSR in 1857, served for 26 years in that capacity, and left behind a stud of hardy 4-4-0s, some of which ran until the 1920s. One of his o/c 4-4-0s, still numbered GNSR 45A, appeared with a train of early GNSR carriages at the Stockton & Darlington Centenary celebrations of 1925. Despite talk of preservation, the engine was

broken up that year. During its GNSR career No 45 enjoyed a lengthy spell as branch engine at Meldrum, where it was well known locally as MELDRUM MEG.

METROPOLITAN TANKS

Legion in number and type, METROPOLITAN TANKS were all designed to cope with problems which were inherent in London suburban traffic, especially where occasional, or prolonged, foray underground was involved. The first were o/c 4-4-0Ts, as supplied to the Metropolitan Railway by Beyer Peacock & Co in 1864. Specially designed for their job, these excellent little tanks could condense their own exhaust, a vital requirement in London's extensive underground system. The Met ultimately acquired 120 of these tanks by 1886, and they handled Inner Circle traffic exclusively until the line was electrified in 1905. Their unqualified success persuaded the LNWR, LSWR and MR to adopt the type for working similar London services of their own, and a variation of the

METROPOLITAN TANK No 22, supplied by Beyer Peacock in 1866, was fitted for oil burning in October 1921. This equipment was removed, however, by the time the locomotive was sold for £300 to the District Railway, where it became No L35, in 1925. *Steamchest*

This remarkable GWR broad gauge METROPOLITAN TANK, *Locust*, emerged from the Vulcan Foundry's Newton-le-Willows workshops (Works No 489) in August 1862. Gooch's last design, 22 such monsters worked the Metropolitan Railway, with no great success, until working arrangements between the GWR and the Met ceased in 1863. *Locust* worked subsequently on GWR London local services, and was withdrawn from stock in June 1877. *Author's Collection*

and a variation of the design even found itself working suburban traffic in Australia.

The GWR, meanwhile, had evolved its own type of METROPOLITAN TANK. Entrusted from January 1863 with the task of operating the broad gauge tracks on the Met between Paddington and Farringdon Street, Gooch introduced a total of 22 2-4-0Ts. They were the first engines in Great Britain to be fitted with condensing apparatus, and, incidentally, the only GWR broad gauge engines to have outside cylinders. Swindon built 10 of them, Vulcan and Kitson supplied the remainder. Notwithstanding the fact that the GWR and the Met decided to go their own separate ways as from August 1863, the broad gauge tanks were not a success. Latterly the GWR altered seven of them to tender engines, and the last of the breed vanished in 1877.

Meanwhile, the GWR had evolved a second type of METROPOLITAN TANK for its own standard gauge use. This was a single-framed 2-4-0T, designed by William Dean, and 140 of them were built between 1869 and 1899 The new GWR tanks performed with undimmed success on suburban services over a long period of years; 116 survived the Grouping, and 10 even lived to enter BR ownership. The last of these hardy little tanks was not seen until 1949.

The GNR, another company faced with tunnel problems in London, adopted 0-4-2, and, latterly, 0-4-4 wheel arrangements for its METROPOLITAN TANKS. Sturrock introduced 20 outside-framed 0-4-2WTs, built by the Avonside Engine Co and Neilson & Co, in 1865-67. All were subsequently reboilered by Patrick Stirling, and the longest survivor lived to November 1905.

Inside frames were the order of the day when Stirling introduced his version of the same design, by having 13 0-4-2WTs turned out from Doncaster Works in 1868-71. Five of these 5 ft 6 in tanks lasted into First World War years, and the last, No 122, was withdrawn in November 1918. Stirling next graduated to 0-4-4 back tanks, and 46 of these were shopped from Doncaster between 1878 and 1881. The only one to reach the Grouping was No 533, withdrawn in 1905 and subsequently converted for use as a crane tank at Doncaster Works, lasting as such until November 1928. Finally, in 1884 Stirling brought in the first of his 0-4-4 side tanks; three classes, 'G1', 'G3' and 'G4', were created by 1895. Short, fast underground runs, with frequent stops and steep gradients, were the daily diet of these superb little engines, and because of their sharp staccato bark they were known generally as WOLVES. The 'G1s', the most powerful of the three classes, were additionally nicknamed DREAD-NOUGHTS (qv).

When W.G. Beattie and the LSWR wondered what type of locomotive to employ on their new Plymouth extension, Beyer Peacock & Co suggested the use of 4-4-0Ts based on the Metropolitan Railway's successful design. Six were duly supplied in 1875. Alas, they proved to be totally unsuitable for Plymouth service, and were rough riders indeed. In the course of the ensuing inquiry, Beyer offered to convert the tanks into tender locomotives; but when the LSWR Board learned that Beattie had been genuinely negligent in employing Beyer MET TANKS in the first place, the suggestion was turned down. The offending tanks were then transferred to the Epsom–Leatherhead service, whence, ironically, they gained considerable popularity with London area crews. All finished up again on West Country duties before the class finally disappeared in 1913. These engines were also known as the PLYMOUTH TANKS.

Lastly, the nickname METROPOLITANS was also applied, rather scornfully, by Scottish crews to LNER Class 'N2' 0-6-2Ts—see BULLDOGS.

MICKEY MOUSES

A somewhat ungrammatical, and derisory, nickname applied by locomen, accustomed to larger engines, to H.G. Ivatt's dainty LMSR 2-6-2Ts and Class '2' MT 2-6-0s. None the less, locomotives of these two useful and numerous classes could be found latterly working all over the BR system. See also WATH DAISIES.

MIDLANDS
See COMPOUNDS.

MIKES
In BR's Eastern Region resident shunting yard engines were, and still are, referred to as MIKES.

MINERS' FRIENDS
A self-explanatory nickname for the LMSR's famous 'Royal Scot' 4-6-0s. Even when rebuilt by Stanier with taper boilers, their firing on major main-line duties still demanded considerable effort. Two, including the prototype, No 46100, have been preserved.

Gresley's massive new LNER 'Mikado', No 2001 *Cock o' the North*, was allocated to Haymarket shed, Edinburgh, from July 1934 until it was rebuilt as an 'A2/2 'Pacific' in September 1944. Much as Haymarket men admired No 2001's prowess on the Aberdeen route, its appetite for coal soon also earned this locomotive the nickname 'MINERS' FRIEND'.

MOGUL
William Adams's last design for the GER before he left for Nine Elms in January 1878 introduced the 2-6-0, or 'Mogul', type to Britain. Fifteen were built for the GER by Neilson & Co in 1878-79, thus entering traffic under Massey Bromley's aegis. Nominally considered more powerful than any other GER engine, they were employed mainly on heavy mineral traffic between Peterborough and London. First No 527, then No 539, worked with the legend MOGUL proudly painted on the driving splasher. Heavy on coal, however, and poorish steamers, locomotives of the class were progressively withdrawn as they required heavy boiler repairs. Two went in 1885, six in 1886, and the remainder were scrapped the following year.

MONGOLIPERS
See WOOLWORTHS.

Despite the prominently displayed legend MOGUL, GER 2-6-0 No 539 and her 14 sisters proved to be a disappointment on heavy London–Peterborough mineral traffic. Supplied by Neilson & Co in 1878-79, the last of the MOGULS, including No 539, were scrapped in 1887. *O. J. Morris*

MOTOR TANKS

F.W. Webb's 4 ft 6 in 2-4-2Ts, built original-ly for LNWR local traffic, were later found to be ideal for motor-train working, and many were motor-fitted from 1909 onwards (see CHOPPERS). A later series, built in 1890-97 with 5 ft 6 in driving wheels, proved equally adaptable, and 42 of that class were motor-fitted by the LMSR during 1927-32. Of the two classes, however, only 41 of the 5 ft 6 in engines survived to be allocated BR numbers.

MOURNERS

See STUPID Ds.

MR DRUMMOND'S CAR

See THE BUG.

MRS JOHNSON

This was a much earlier version of the BANTAM HEN situation (qv), this time on the OW&WR. Two small 2-2-2 o/c well tanks of very elaborate appearance were sup-plied by R. Stephenson & Co in 1859. They had inside frames, ornamental domes and large caps with side windows. Numbered 52 and 53, the first bore the name *Ben Johnson*. Later, as GWR engines, they worked the Chipping Norton branch, whence the unnamed locomotive became known locally as MRS JOHNSON. Both were withdrawn by 1878.

N

NAGS and NODDIES.

The application of nicknames spilled over, of course, into the diesel era. NAGS was the nickname applied by BR men to the new 350 hp diesel shunting locomotives, and so, too, was the term DONKEYS. The name NODDIES was bestowed by BR men on small 100 hp diesel shunters.

NEDDIES

Here we have a series of six 0-6-0Ts, built by Sharp Stewart & Co and introduced by the FR in 1867-73. Used for banking on joint lines in the Cleator Moor area, these engines had long side tanks which, stretching almost to the front of the smokebox, created, when seen from the front, some resemblance to horses' blinkers, hence the nickname NEDDIES. Four which survived the Grouping were classified '2F' by the LMSR. But life was short, and the last, No 11552, was scrapped in June 1926.

OBAN BOGIES

The original OBAN BOGIES were 10 o/c 4-4-0s which were built by Dubs & Co in 1882 to the order of G. Brittain for the specific purpose of handling traffic on the CR's steeply-graded Oban line. Front end apart, they were similar to the HR's SKYE BOGIES (qv). The OBAN BOGIES proved to be equally useful and capable engines, particularly during heavy holiday seasons, and an interesting feature was the provision of four-wheeled tenders, to assist in weight reduction. In the event they soldiered on until they were replaced at the turn of the century by a second generation, this time of the 4-6-0 wheel arrangement. Three of the 4-4-0s survived to carry LMSR numbers, but were scrapped in 1930.

The second OBAN BOGIES, J.F. McIntosh's first 4-6-0 design, made their debut in 1902, and provided a much needed increase in power and adhesion. The first i/c six-coupled express locomotives in the UK, five were built in 1902, and four more followed in 1905. Again a small tender was provided, six-wheeled on this occasion, but modest enough not to require increased turntable facilities. Withdrawals began in 1928. Two were rebuilt with larger boilers in 1930, and the last survivor, LMS No 14606,

perished in November 1937.

OLD FAITHFUL

When D.E. Marsh more or less copied H.A. Ivatt's GNR design, the five 'Atlantics' that Kitson & Co built for the LB&SCR in 1905-06 were an instant success. Five years later, March's successor, L. Billinton, acting with initial caution, had six superheated 'Atlantics' built at Brighton, and these, too, were proudly hailed by LB&SCR men. The Kitson five were all withdrawn by July 1951, but the others continued in quite vigorous service. No 32421 *South Foreland*, for example, was officially 'in store' by late 1952; yet, on 5 and 19 October that year it was earmarked for standby duty on RCTS 'Atlantic Specials', as well as performing other quite strenuous routine duties. Many of the shed staff at Brighton held the engine in high regard as OLD FAITHFUL, and must have been vexed when it was withdrawn in August 1956 with a track record of well over one million miles.

OLD FIREWORKS

Early electric locomotives also perpetuated the tradition of nicknames. The Great Northern & City Railway, opened on 13 February 1904, was worked for three years by the contractors, S. Pearson & Son Ltd, and it was the latter who ordered 35 sets of electrical traction and control equipment from BTH Ltd. As only 32 of the sets were allocated to motor coaches, the opportunity was taken to utilise one of the 'spare' sets in the construction of a shunting locomotive. Used for the movement of dead stock at Drayton Park depot, the 'home-made' loco invariably produced such a pyrotechnic display when moved that it became known, quite affectionately, as OLD FIREWORKS.

OLDHAM INCLINE ENGINES

Built at the L&YR's Miles Platting Works during 1856-71, a series of 26 0-6-0STs, with the saddle tank reaching from the smokebox front to the front of a raised firebox, were specifically designed as passenger engines. Quite often they were referred to as the

OLDHAM INCLINE ENGINES. Withdrawals commenced in the 1880s, and the last, No 361, went to the scrapyard in 1899.

OLD HICCUPS

One of Colonel Stephens's most futile purchases was an 0-8-0T, built new by Hawthorn Leslie & Co for £2,340 in 1905. The engine proved to be a complete 'white elephant' in K&ESR service, and in July 1932 W.H. Austen, Receiver of the K&ESR, parted with it in an exchange deal with the SR. Found to be in reasonably good order, the tank, still bearing its name, *Hecate*, was renumbered 949 in SR stock and spent most of its remaining years performing sundry duties around Nine Elms depot. In 1938 two of her regular crew dubbed the locomotive OLD HICCUPS, because of the faltering nature of her exhaust when working easily. The sturdy old tank was eventually withdrawn in March 1950.

OLD LADIES

J.G. Robinson's first eight-coupled design for the GCR, his Class '8A' 0-8-0s, introduced in 1902, earned immediate popularity with GCR men. Teasingly nicknamed TINIES (qv) because of their size, and OLD LADIES because of their grave demeanour, the 89 which were constructed by 1911 toiled unceasingly in the great coalfield areas, and were always regarded as 'strong' engines. During the First World War 15 of them served in France, and, though overshadowed latterly by the ROD (qv) 2-8-0s, the whole class entered LNER stock as Class 'Q4'. An intention to eliminate the class in 1938 was, happily, thwarted by the outbreak of the Second World War. Thus, the last, BR No 63243, was not withdrawn until October 1951. Meanwhile, 13 OLD LADIES had been rebuilt in 0-8-0T form, LNER Class 'Q1', by Edward Thompson in 1942-45.

The popularity of the GCR's 0-8-0s, nicknamed OLD LADIES and TINIES (qv), did not diminish when Grouping found a new home for many in the GNR Section of the LNER, particularly in the West Riding area. No 5961 was one of a handful which were even spotted around Hornsey in the mid-1920s. *Author's Collection*

OLD SCHOOL TIES
See FOOTBALLERS.

OLD STUMPHY
No 825, the last of 20 o/c 4-6-0s built for the NER in 1911-13, and designed by Vincent Raven, emerged from Darlington Works with cylinders of 'Uniflow' design and Walschaerts valve gear. The design was the idea of Professor Stumpf of Berlin, and the engine, bizarre in appearance and possessed of an abnormally loud exhaust, became known to NER men as OLD STUMPHY. The cylinders gave considerable trouble, and, rebuilt along conventional Class 'S2' lines in 1924, the locomotive was eventually withdrawn by the LNER in February 1944.

ORANGE BOXES
Sacré's last design before resigning from active MS&LR service was a shunting tank, known as Class '7', and six of these 0-6-0Ts were built at Gorton Works in 1895. They had long angular side tanks which extended from cab to smokebox, with no access whatever to the inside motion. This boxlike appearance led to them being nicknamed ORANGE BOXES, or PIANO TANKS, and the last pair were scrapped shortly after the Grouping, in March and July 1923. Withdrawn from Wrexham, they had been highly regarded there by ex-GCR men.

OUTSIDE SWINGERS
The last class of 0-6-0 subscribed by A. Sturrock before his early departure from GNR Locomotive Engineer service in October 1866, in favour of Patrick Stirling, was a series of 70 Class '400' outside-framed locomotives. All were supplied by various well-known British locomotive manufacturers between January 1865 and May 1866. Meanwhile, at Sturrock's insistence, the first 20, Nos 400-19, were equipped with auxiliary

NER 4-6-0 No 825, commonly known as OLD STUMPHY, was, until 1919, the sole British example of Prof Stumpf's 'Uniflow' system of steam distribution. Although the Stumpf system was quite commonly employed on the Continent, lengthy trials with No 825 ended with the locomotive being rebuilt in conventional form at Darlington Works in 1924. *Author's Collection*

steam tenders to 'assist' them in working heavy main-line coal trains between London and Peterborough. Before long, what with excessive cab heat and rough riding, GNR locomen and fitters soon learned to hate Sturrock's innovation. Withdrawals of the '400' Class began in June 1896 with No 440 (Neilson & Co, Works No 1171/1866) and ended in October 1908 with No 435 (Kitson & Co, Works No 1280/1865). The introduction of modern inside-framed 0-6-0s saw the old outside-framed Sturrock types rather contemptuously referred to as OUTSIDE SWINGERS.

P

PACKET OF WOODBINES

When ten of George Hughes's extremely handsome 4-6-4Ts were completed by the LMSR in 1924 they were given Nos 11110-19. At that stage of British life, cigarettes were commonly sold in packets of five (for 2d!), and it seemed quite natural for some L&YR wag to coin the nickname PACKET OF WOODBINES when referring to No 11111. Built in March 1924, poor old 11111 was withdrawn in January 1940.

PADDLE BOXES

See DOUBLE BREASTERS.

PAGET'S FOLLY

This nickname was the fruit of extraordinary events at Derby Works in 1908. R.M. Deeley was the MR Locomotive Superintendent at the time. Cecil Paget had just been appointed General Superintendent, and, despite Deeley's misgivings, authority was given to implement a private order to construct a revolutionary 2-6-2 i/c locomotive which Paget had designed. Building of the engine, which had no fewer than eight single-acting cylinders, 18 in x 12 in, with rotary steam distribution valves, ruined Paget financially, and the MR had to contribute additional funds to

ensure its completion. In the event PAGET'S FOLLY, as the engine was latterly known, never entered traffic. The project was abandoned, and the locomotive was finally broken up in 1920.

PAINT POT

A unique 3 ft 1½ in gauge vertical boilered locomotive which was built in the 1870s by A.F. Craig & Co, Paisley, for use in the firm's own foundry. Two 6 in x 8 in vertical cylinders supplied geared power, and 'steering wheels' fitted at the boiler end took the locomotive round extremely acute bends. Highly successful, and rebuilt several times, the strange contraption carried the nickname PAINT POT right to the end of its career in 1966, when a petrol-driven tractor took over.

PATRIOTS

See BABY SCOTS.

PEACOCKS

Thirty Class 'J3' 4-4-0s, built by Beyer Peacock for the L&YR in 1888-89, were so typically stylish in appearance that Lanky men always referred to them proudly as PEACOCKS. Good reliable engines, all but four survived the Grouping, and the last, LMSR No 10123, was not withdrawn until December 1934.

The same nickname was applied by M&GNJR men to a smaller series of 15 Class 'A' 4-4-0s, also supplied by Beyer Peacock, in 1882-88. In due course all were rebuilt with standard MR boilers, and five of them were added to LNER stock in 1936. Still popular with locomen, they worked away on their home territory until the last, No 025, went to the breakers in May 1941.

PEARSON NINE-FOOTERS

These were eight extraordinary, yet quite beautiful, 4-2-4 well and back tank broad gauge express engines which were built by Rothwell & Co in 1853-54. They were designed by J. Pearson, Company Engineer to the Bristol & Exeter Railway, and one time Atmospheric Superintendent on the South Devon Railway. These engines had 9-foot

The classic lines of the PEACOCK are clearly evident in this view. Built in 1883 by Beyer Peacock (Works No 2340) for the Eastern & Midlands Railway, this 4-4-0 later entered M&GNJR stock as Class 'A' No 27. Renumbered 027 by the LNER in November 1936, it was withdrawn three months later. *Author's Collection*

driving wheels, and in the event they handled Exeter expresses with great expedition. The highest recorded speed of a NINE-FOOTER was 81.8 mph down Wellington Bank. Oddly enough, they did not enjoy a long life, and all were withdrawn, or replaced, before the GWR took over in January 1876.

PET OF THE LINE
See THE BUG.

PIANO FRONTS
A series of 4-cyl compound 0-8-0s, introduced by F.W. Webb for the LNWR in 1901, soon acquired the nickname PIANO FRONTS because of the prominent valve cover they sported below the smokebox. Classified 'B', 170 were built by 1904. The first withdrawal, in 1921, was occasioned by a boiler explosion, and the last survivor was scrapped in 1928. Prior to that, 36 of them had been converted to 2-8-0 compounds, to

relieve the overhang in front. The remainder were altered, to become 2-cyl simple 0-8-0s of the 'G1' Class. See also BILL BAILEYS.

PIANO TANKS
See ORANGE BOXES.

PILLING PIG
When the Garstang & Knott End Railway commenced initial services in December 1870, it relied on one hired locomotive. Reconstituted latterly, the Company employed a few more engines, but these were never numbered. One 0-6-0ST, supplied by Hudswell Clarke & Rodgers in 1875, carried the name *Farmers Friend*, but the sound of its whistle, said to resemble the dying throes of a pig, soon earned it the local nickname of the PILLING PIG. The engine was sold in 1900, and was replaced by another Hudswell 0-6-0ST, named, this time rather grandiloquently, *New Century*.

PLYMOUTH TANKS
See METROPOLITAN TANKS.

PNEUMONIA ENGINES
NER men, like NBR crews, were well accustomed to roomy and comfortable cabs, and it follows that when a number of GCR-type 'O4' 2-8-0s were posted to York in early post-Grouping days their draughty, unsheltered cabs were highly unpopular. Thus, at York, the 'O4s', though appreciated well enough for their power and tenacity, were dubbed PNEUMONIA ENGINES by ex-NER locomen.

POLKAS
These were Stephenson 'long boilered' 2-4-0s which were purchased by the MR in 1846-48. Inside frames and haystack fireboxes were common to the class, which came from various makers, and all wheels were placed in front of the firebox. The latter feature, coupled in this instance with outside cylinders, generated an uncomfortable swaying motion which earned these locomotives their nickname, the source of which was a popular dance which had just been introduced to Britain. Ten were rebuilt as 2-2-2s and 14 as 2-4-0s, all with inside cylinders, not long after the class was introduced. The remaining four were rebuilt by Kitson & Co as 0-6-0s, and one of these, No 757, was the last to be broken up, in June 1868.

POM POMS
These powerful and popular 0-6-0s were designed by J.G. Robinson in 1901, and were his first goods design for the GCR. In all 174 were built by 1910. Immediately they were introduced they became known as POM POMS, for the sharp bark of their exhaust reminded men of the quick-firing gun of that name which had been used in the South African War. Great favourites with locomen, the POM POMS could work anything from pick-up goods to express trains; and appropriate compliment was paid to the class, by then 'J11', when Edward Thompson selected them as one of the LNER's standard post-Second World War types. Many witnessed the demise of steam in the UK, and one of many variations, a piston-valved engine, BR No 64354, was last to bow the knee in October 1962.

PONIES
See TAMBOURINIES.

POTATO CANS
Aware, through experience, of the defects of steam railcars on the LSWR, Dugald Drummond, in 1906, ordered 10 small 2-2-0Ts at £875 each from Nine Elms Works. With high boilers and short wheelbase, the tiny locomotives looked as tall as they were long. Limited tractive effort, alas, produced a propensity for slipping, and soon they became known, derisively, as POTATO CANS or ROCKETS. In 1913 Urie order five to be rebuilt as four-coupled tanks, with the others to be withdrawn as they required heavy repairs. In the event seven were sold during the First World War, and three, in 0-4-0T form, passed to the SR, then to BR. The last, working as Engineer's Department No 77S, carried on until April 1959.

PRECURSOR TANKS
These were 50 LNWR 4-4-2Ts which were designed by G. Whale along the lines of his successful 'Precursor' 4-4-0 express engines. Built in 1906-09, the new locomotives rode unsteadily at first, because of the volume of water in the side tanks. Once this defect was overcome, however, they proved to be highly useful engines. They certainly impressed LB&SCR men, who came across them at Willesden on 'Sunny South Express' workings; and LMSR suburban services out of Euston were almost monopolised by the PRECURSOR TANKS until LMSR standard 2-6-4Ts arrived in 1932. The last two, Nos 6790 and 6824, were scrapped in February 1940.

PRIDE OF HORNSEY
For decades Stirling and Ivatt 0-6-0STs were an integral part of the GNR scene around London. King's Cross, Finsbury Park, Ludgate Hill—all were haunts of these busy, sturdy

Drummond's LSWR Class 'C14' motor-tanks, the POTATO CANS, had chequered careers. No 741, seen here at Eastleigh in SR guise, was one of three which survived to enter BR stock. It was withdrawn as BR No 30588 in December 1957. *Author's Collection*

little tanks, and for years prior to the Second World War Hornsey shed kept one of the 'J52' Class in particularly pristine condition. Known locally as the PRIDE OF HORNSEY, No 4252 was employed mainly on East London goods transfer duties. Built at Doncaster in 1901, she lasted to May 1957. Two years later, King's Cross saw the very last of the saddle tanks it had held in such great affection.

PRIDE OF LONDON

This nickname was applied to No 2665, an LNER Class 'N2' 0-6-2T which was built by Hawthorn Leslie & Co (Works No 3694) in November 1928. The locomotive was allocated to King's Cross shed, and was kept in immaculate condition by the two crews who manned her regularly. This high standard was maintained right into the immediate post-Second World War years, when locomotive maintenance was still at a very low ebb; no doubt the PRIDE OF LONDON, by now BR

No 69571, still shone brightly when it met its doom in June 1961.

PRINCE TANKS

The earliest use of the PRINCE TANK nickname occurred when C.J. Bowen Cooke, of the LNWR, shopped his 5 ft 6 in 4-6-2 passenger tanks in 1911-16. Forty-seven were built, mostly superheated as new. Wrongly assumed to be a tank version of the LNWR's 'Prince of Wales' 4-6-0, and consequently frequently referred to as PRINCE TANKS, these handsome 'Pacific' tanks were the first LNWR engines to be built new with the Belpair firebox. All lasted until well after the Grouping, and a solitary survivor, No 6979, was not withdrawn until April 1941.

Introduced on the LMSR in 1927, Fowler's 2-cyl 2-6-4Ts were also handsome engines, and their appearance alone seemed to justify the nickname PRINCE TANKS by which they were known to some railway enthusiasts. In fact, this nickname simply arose from the fact that one of the class, No 2313, was temporarily named *The Prince* when the Prince of Wales happened to visit Derby Works in 1928. The name was removed when the engine was first repainted, but the nickname lingered on a while longer.

PRINCESS MARY
See MARY.

PUFFING BILLY
See BLACK BILLY.

PUGS
Often PUGS were dock shunting engines, as in L&YR parlance. In Scotland, however, *all* tank engines, whether saddle or side tank and regardless of the duties involved, were known as PUGS.

PUMPERS
Peter Drummond introduced a massive Class '71' 0-6-0 on the G&SWR in 1913. All 15 were built by NBL and, although not superheated, they were, at 58 tons, the heaviest of their type in Great Britain. Apart from introducing left-hand drive, very much a Drummond hallmark, the '71s' were fitted with feed pumps, hence their nickname PUMPERS. They were loathed by G&SWR men. A myriad of water tubes below the tender leaked constantly, and it is somewhat surprising that these engines did not attract the nickname which was later thrust upon the undeserving LMSR BABY SCOTS (qv), ie WATERCARTS. Although good enough steamers, the PUMPERS were sluggish on gradients, and their big ends were chronically prone to overheating. The latter vice was later cured by replacing the marine-type big ends with a cottered type of bearing. But coal consumption, too, was heavy, and when R.H.Whitelegg arrived at Kilmarnock in 1918 all Drummond 'gadgets'—steam driers, feed pumps and feed water heaters—were removed. As a result, maintenance costs of these engines were drastically reduced. The first batch of PUMPERS to be withdrawn went in 1930, and No 17758, the last survivor, met its end in September 1933.

PUPS
See TERRIERS.

QUEEN MARY
See MARY.

R

RACEHORSES
When the ECR took over the Newmarket Railway's total motive power in November 1850 it was found to consist of five o/c 0-6-0 tender engines which had been built by Gilkes Wilkinson & Co two years earlier. All were named after famous racehorses of the time, and for a while the locomotives were employed, somwhat uncharacteristically, on coal trains between Peterborough and Stratford. Never rebuilt, and inevitably nicknamed RACEHORSES, the whole class was broken up by 1870.

The other famous RACEHORSES were, of course, Gresley's immortal LNER 'Pacifics' of 1923-25.

RAGTIMERS
When Nigel Gresley introduced his new MT 2-6-0s to the GNR in 1920 he employed the Walschaerts valve gear, and the distinctive noise made by the nickel-chrome steel connecting and coupling rods soon led to the locomotives being nicknamed RAGTIMERS. Ten were built at Doncaster in 1912, and 65 engines of the 'K2' Class followed in 1913-21. A few years after the Grouping, 13 'K2s' were sent to the West Highland line, where, carrying the names of Scottish lochs, they worked successfully for many years. The 'K2s' were regarded in Scotland as good engines 'at heart', but their

Despite their RAGTIMER and TIN LIZZIE nicknames, Gresley's 5 ft 8 in 2-6-0s served the GNR, LNER and BR well. Seen here at Perth on 4 June 1960, No 61788 *Loch Rannoch*, a Kitson & Co product (Works No 5348) of August 1921, was withdrawn exactly one year later. *Steamchest*

rough riding, right-hand drive, pull-out regulator and poorly sheltered cabs were all alien to ex-NBR men. It follows that as the Model T Ford car, equally unsophisticated in design, had become highly popular by then, the nickname TIN LIZZIES also heartfeltly attached itself to Scottish Area 'K2s'. None the less withdrawals of the 'K2s' did not commence until 1955, but by 1962 the last, No 61756, a Doncaster veteran of 1918, had gone.

RAMSBOTTOM EXPRESS ENGINES
See IRONCLADS.

RATTLERS
See BROAD STREET RATTLERS.

READING GOODS
Standard goods engines were initiated on the SER in 1856, when four powerful 0-6-0s, designed by J. Cudworth, energed from Ashford Works. Cudworth favoured a 'long boiler' type, but on this occasion he was over-ruled by his Locomotive Committee. Early employment found for the 0-6-0s on the steeply-graded Redhill–Reading branch gave them their nickname. By now coke-burning was also being viewed with disfavour, and Cudworth responded by fitting coal-burning fireboxes to a second batch of READING GOODS, which were built, again at Ashford, between 1859 and 1876, the year of his resignation. Latterly the Cudworth engines were superceded by James Stirling's new Class 'O' 0-6-0s. Accordingly, the first READING GOODS withdrawal took place in 1883, and October 1904 saw the last of them.

REBUILT RIVERS
R.E.L. Maunsell pioneered the 2-6-4T type on the SE&CR in 1917 with his 'K' Class No 790; 19 more were added by the SR during 1925-26. Despite misgivings on the part of the SR's Running Department, more still would have been built—had not No A800 of the species come a fearful cropper at Sevenoaks on 21 August 1927. Thirteen lives

were lost in that accident, and, much to the SR's discomfiture, enquiry evidence of the derailment incited a rather vulgar newspaper headline, the 'Rolling Rivers'. Pending the results of subsequent trials, which were conducted by Nigel Gresley on the LNER main line, the SR withdrew the entire class from traffic. In the event, Gresley's tests cast aspersions both on the springing of the 2-6-4Ts and the vulnerability of SR track. Thus, SR management, anxious to put the incident behind them, opted to rebuild all the 'K' tanks as 2-6-0 tender engines. This was duly effected in 1928, when Nos A790-809 were reclassified 'U'. Alas, SR enginemen rather confounded Company psychology by insisting on referring to the original 20 as REBUILT RIVERS. The melancholy association was only finally broken when No 31791, formerly 2-6-4T River Adur, went to the breakers in June 1966. Meanwhile, 'U' Class No 31806, formerly River Torridge, was rescued from Barry scrapyard, and now functions happily on the Mid Hants Railway. See also U BOATS.

RED DEVILS

MR and LMSR compound 4-4-0s were loved by some locomen, and loathed by others. The latter, no doubt, were amongst those who knew these remarkably pugnacious engines as RED DEVILS! See also COMPOUNDS and CRIMSON RAMBLERS.

RED STANIERS
See JUBILEES.

RETFORD PACIFICS

In 1909-10 H.A. Ivatt introduced 20 Class 'J22' 0-6-0s in a bid to meet the GNR's rapidly increasing goods and coal traffic. The LNER classified them 'J35', and shortly after the Grouping the whole class moved to Retford shed. There they soon became affectionately known as the RETFORD PACIFICS. The nickname was probably a good-natured allusion to the fact that most other main LNER sheds had their own allocation of Gresley 4-6-2s. Ironically, in practice the Retford 'J5s' often had to turn out to replace failed 'Pacifics'! They certainly were doughty

RETFORD PACIFIC No 3024 (Doncaster Works No 1269/1910) was allocated to Doncaster shed during 1940-42, whence it and the rest of the class moved on to the Nottingham area. One of two last survivors, it was withdrawn in December 1955 as BR No 65483. *Author's Collection*

old engines, and all saw in the 1950s, with the last two, Nos 65483 and 65498, going together in December 1955.

ROBERT THE DEVIL

This nickname was given by GCR men to Sacré's first six-wheeled single not long after it was shopped from Gorton Works in 1882, and was inspired by the fact that inclined outside cylinders and a short wheelbase combined to produce an unsteady 'hunting' motion at even reasonable speeds. Subsequent engines of the class, 11 in number, were modified accordingly, and, although still lively locomotives, they spent the next 20 years operating fast passenger services on the Cheshire lines.

ROCKETS

See POTATO CANS.

RODs

While the Railway Operating Department of

the War Office 'borrowed' over 600 locomotives of various types from no fewer than 13 British railway companies during the early years of the First World War, there can be no doubt that the 'classic' ROD engine was J.G. Robinson's earlier GCR 2-8-0, later LNER class 'O4'—in reality a development of his 0-8-0s (see TINIES). The '8Ks', as they were classified on the GCR, were introduced in 1911, and thanks to their straightforward design they achieved instant popularity; 130 were built by the GCR before the Grouping. Chosen additionally as a standard type by the Ministry of Munitions in 1917, and thus styled type 'MM' (see MAGGIE MURPHIES), 521 more were built by the GCR and sundry private contractors for use in the theatre of war. When hostilities ceased in 1919 many were sold to British railway companies, amongst them the GWR, LNWR and, later, LNER. Some went as far afield as China. Meanwhile, the large number absorbed by the LNER in 1924-29 made

The ROD. When J.G. Robinson introduced his 2-8-0 design on the GCR in 1911 no one could have visualised the historical role these engines would play over the next 55 years. No 405, seen here at Nottingham on 9 July 1923, was one of the original 30 which were shopped from Gorton in 1911-12. It survived to be withdrawn as BR No 63669 in November 1960. *Steamchest*

them easily that railway's largest class. A considerable complement which were ultimately allocated to Mexborough shed emulated Retford shed practice by being nicknamed MEXBOROUGH PACIFICS. In Fife and Aberdeen the LNER 'O4s' were known respectively as BIG AGGIES and TIN LIZZIES.

Came the Second World War, and again large numbers of ROD 2-8-0s went overseas, some for the second time in their lives. Many did not return to the UK, but in 1948, by which time several rebuilds had been undertaken, 219 Class 'O4s' passed into BR hands. Serious withdrawals began in 1959, and by 1965 the various sub-classes were extinct. Fortunately a move to preserve No 63601 as part of the National Collection was consummated in 1963, and the locomotive can presently be seen at the Dinting Railway Centre.

It is also interesting to note that while an original Robinson 2-8-0, built at Glasgow in 1911, cost £4,500, the price of a similar locomotive rose to £6,030 by 1917, and £10,000 by 1919. See also FROGGIES.

ROOTERS
See TERRIERS.

ROWLANDS
These were the locomotives operated by Christopher Rowlands, who handled contract work at Swansea Harbour until the Swansea Harbour Trust was formed in 1905. Of the 13 engines he employed, eight were Peckett standard 0-4-0STs. Only eight of Rowland's more modern locos were retained by the SHT, and these bore brass plates on which the running number was prefixed by 'R'. Four of the Peckett tanks changed hands when the GWR absorbed the Swansea Harbour Trust on 1 July 1923, and the last survivor, GWR No 926, a veteran of 1899, was sold in July 1929.

S

SALMON TINS
A popular, and not unaffectionate, nickname for small-boilered LNWR 0-6-0 tender engines.

SANDIES
This was the nickname by which the LNER 'Sandringham' Class 4-6-0s were known in East Anglia. But see also FOOTBALLERS.

SANDWICHES
See SCOTCHMEN.

SCHARNHORST and GNEISENAU
Of the ill-fated 'River' Class 4-6-0s which were built to the order of F.G. Smith in 1915, ostensibly for service on the HR, but sold latterly to the CR (see HIELMEN), only two survived the onset of the Second World War. Bearing LMSR Nos 14758 and 14760 by then, both 'Rivers' served in the Ayr locality during the war years. Quite the most massive engines ever seen working locally, they eventually acquired the nicknames SCHARNHORST and GNEISENAU, after the two German cruisers which made such a spectacular dash through the English Channel, from Brest to Kiel, in February 1942. Local Ayrshire vernacular soon translated the nickname GNEISENAU into JEANNIE SHAW. In the event, No 14758 went to the breakers in September 1945, and dear old JEANNIE SHAW followed suit in December 1946.

SCOTCHMEN
Robert Sinclair's last locomotives for the GER, 20 2-4-2 well tanks, were built by Neilson & Co of Glasgow in 1864-65, thus earning this nickname. Employed initially on Enfield services, they were ungainly looking engines, with a long low boiler, tall stovepipe chimney, outside cylinders, driving wheel splashers and very small bunkers. Notoriously unpopular with GER men, the last was scrapped in 1888.

No 58326's class nickname, SALMON TINS, was not derisory in any way, for these small-boilered LNWR 0-6-0s were held in great respect. Webb 'Coal Engine' No 58326, withdrawn by BR in May 1853, had started life nearly 80 years previously as Crewe-built LNWR No 986. *Author's Collection*

Translated from GNEISENAU to JEANNIE SHAW in the local vernacular, ex-CR 4-6-0 No 14760 prepares to leave Inverness. This locomotive, taken out of service in April 1939, but reinstated 18 months later, was eventually withdrawn, as the last of the species, in December 1946. *Steamchest*

Also nicknamed SCOTCHMEN, because they, too, were built by Neilson & Co, 14 robust double-framed 0-4-2 well tanks were introduced by W.Martley of the LC&DR in 1866. Their mission in life was to operate LC&DR running powers which had been granted by the Metropolitan Railway. Known additionally as SANDWICHES, because of their limited footplate space, they had double spectacle cab sheets and condensing equipment, and were named after Scottish islands and rivers, which consolidated their nickname. By the mid-1870s, however, suburban loads were beginning to exceed the capabilities of the SCOTCHMEN, and they were progressively replaced by larger, more powerful Kirtley 0-4-4WTs. The last SCOTCHMAN was not withdrawn, nevertheless, until May 1900. In the meantime, a slightly larger version, also Neilson-built, was introduced in 1873, and, again given romantic Celtic names, they were known popularly as LARGE SCOTCHMEN.

The LB&SCR also had their complement of SCOTCHMEN—see BUSTERS.

SCOTSMEN
SCOTSMEN were a much more modern proposition. Early in 1925 the SR, having just completed 10 'improved' 'King Arthur' Class 4-6-0s at Eastleigh, opted to order 30 more, at £10,085 apiece, from NBL of Hyde Park Works, Glasgow. The opportunity was taken to specify the fitting of Ashford cabs and smokebox doors, plus large Urie tenders. All were named after Knights of the Round Table, and, quickly put into service, these engines gained an excellent reputation as the SCOTSMEN. Withdrawals did not commence until late 1959, and No 30077 *Sir Lamiel*, removed from Basingstoke shed in 1961, was later added to the National Collection. It might be added that 'King Arthurs' were also the subject of early SR experiments in dealing with smoke problems, and were the first locomotives in the UK to be fitted with what later became standard smoke deflectors. Large-diameter fabricated chimneys, with built-in spark arresters, were also fitted experimentally to one or two during

1947-50, and 'King Arthurs' fitted thus automatically assumed a portly bearing which gave rise to a new nickname, the BEEFEATERS.

SCOTTIES
Neilson & Co of Glasgow and the Vulcan Foundry of Newton-le-Willows shared in the provision of 28 0-6-0 tender engines to the S&DJR over the years 1870-90. Only the first batch came from Glasgow, but that was enough for S&DJR men to dub the whole class SCOTTIES. Eleven duly passed into LMSR hands at the Grouping, but all had vanished by December 1932.

SCOTTISH DIRECTORS
See DIRECTORS.

SCOTTS
Here we have a generic term which covered unsuperheated and superheated Class 'J' NBR 4-4-0s, 43 of which, designed by W.P. Reid, were built, mostly at Cowlairs Works, between the years 1909 and 1920. Taken into LNER stock as Classes 'D29' and 'D30', all were in fact superheated within a year or two. Thirty-seven were taken over by BR in due course, but, while the last 'D29' went in 1952, extinction of the 'D30s' was held off until 1960. The nickname SCOTTS arose from the fact that all were named after novels and characters created by Sir Walter Scott.

SCRAP TANKS
The HR's works at Lochgorm built 41 locomotives before construction ceased there in 1906. Output for 1903-04 was particularly interesting, consisting, as it did, of three 0-6-0Ts, which were classified 'V' by the HR. Modest o/c tanks, with 5 ft 2½ in driving wheels, they were constructed from parts which had been salvaged from withdrawn 2-4-0 passenger locomotives; thus they fell heir to the nickname SCRAP TANKS. Though primarily intended for shunting duties, one, later LMSR No 16382, performed branch duties for a while. Two were withdrawn in 1930, and No 16381 followed suit two years later. The LMSR classified them 2F.

SEAGULLS

Four 4-4-0s which were supplied to the FR by Sharp Stewart & Co in 1890 were really a bogie version of 2-4-0s which had been introduced 20 years earlier. With separate coupled wheel splashers and an enlarged four-wheeled tender, however, they looked handsome enough to attract the name SEAGULLS. The LMSR, though classifying them only as '1P', treated them to a red livery. Alas, the SEAGULLS did not last long as a species, and the last, No 10133, was withdrawn in October 1927.

SEA PIGS

After the Grouping, most ex-GNR 0-8-0s (see LONG TOMS), displaced by ex-ROD (qv) 2-8-0s, gravitated towards the Colwick and Ardsley districts. Some worked a night goods to Hull, whence their inordinate appetite for water caused them to be known locally as SEA PIGS.

The L&YR's rather eccentric 0-8-0s also earned the nickname SEA PIGS because of an addiction to priming, poor water circula-tion, and general sluggishness in steaming. Although many of these 0-8-0s were built between 1904 and 1921, comparatively few survived to enter BR stock in 1948. Of those which did, the last, No 52870, was with-drawn in September 1951.

SEA SICK TANKS

In 1874 William Stroudley tackled a paucity of suitable short-distance goods and yard-piloting locomotives on the LB&SCR by introducing six 0-6-0 'E' tanks. Then in 1880, so critical had the London suburban situation become, Sroudley, having built many more 'E' tanks, applied the temporary expedient of ungrading several to passenger service. In truth, the little tanks had no difficulty in coping with suburban work, but passengers complained of 'surging' and 'bumping', and locomen found great difficulty in firing the Class 'Es' at speed. All in all, they hardly deserved the nickname they earned of SEA SICK TANKS, for all the complaints listed were natural consequences of employing six-

SEAGULL. The handsome lines of the FR's Sharp Stewart 4-4-0s of 1890 are self-evident in this study of No 123. Renumbered 10134 by the LMSR, but only classified '1P', the engine only lasted until September 1925. *Author's Collection*

SEA PIG No 114 was the first (Works No 841) of a final batch of 20 Aspinall 0-8-0s which were turned out by Horwich Works in 1903. Given a Hughes boiler in 1912, it soldiered on as LMSR No 12782 and BR No 52782 until August 1950. *Author's Collection*

coupled light tanks, not designed for the purpose, on fast local passenger work.

SEMIS

At the height of the East/West Coast rivalry of the 1930s, W.A. Stanier played an auspicious card for the LMSR by producing his streamlined 'Coronation' 4-6-2s. They added enormous prestige to the LMSR's non-stop Euston–Glasgow workings; 24 'Streamliners' were eventually built, then production ceased after Stanier's retirement early in 1944. That same year work commenced on 'defrocking' the streamlined 'Pacifics', and the process was completed in May 1949. The finished products, however, could still be distinguished from the other 14 'Coronations' by the tapered smokebox tops they now bore, and they attracted the nickname SEMIS.

SHARPIES

In 1862 Sharp Stewart & Co built 10 beautiful standard gauge single-wheelers for the GWR at the instigation of Daniel Gooch.

Popular and hard-working, they bore little resemblance to the world-famous Sharp singles, but were still nicknamed LITTLE SHARPIES. 'Renewals' were introduced around 1877, and the last of the originals vanished in August 1881.

Some 55 0-6-0s which Sharp Stewart supplied to the FR over the years 1866-84 were also known to locomen as SHARPIES. Many acquired LMSR numbers, but all were withdrawn by 1927.

The GNR also had its quota of SHARPIES (see TAILWAGGERS).

SHED ANCHOR

No 2906 *Lady of Lynn*, a 'Saint' Class 4-6-0 built at Swindon in 1906, spent most of her working life at Canton shed, Cardiff, where she was affectionately known as the SHED ANCHOR. Last of the GWR 'Ladies' to be withdrawn, it was appropriate that she should leave Canton shed one morning in August 1952, well polished, to meet her doom. Her lifetime mileage was 1,903,025.

SHOOTING GALLERIES

This nickname, bestowed on F.W. Webb's remarkable o/c 2-2-2-2 compound locomotives, was, of course, a reflection upon the length of the boiler, which seemed sensational at the time. A second nickname, LONG STOMACHS, was soon also coined by weary LNWR men. The first of these engines, *Greater Britain*, was shopped by Crewe Works in October 1891, and almost everything about her was unorthodox; further engines of the type were not built until two years later. Meanwhile, Webb had taken the unusual course of testing the prototype by causing her to make a round trip from Euston to Carlisle and back every day for a week.

Nine more 6 ft 10 in 'Greater Britain' Class locomotives were added in 1893-94, and both they and 10 similar 6-foot 'John Hick' Class engines which followed in 1894-98 were given double-barrelled names, with one half on each splasher. At the time of Queen Victoria's Diamond Jubilee the LNWR, intensely patriotic, painted the first two 'Greater Britains' Post Office red and creamy white respectively. Only one of these divided drive compounds, however, No 1505 *Richard Arkwright*, lingered as long as May 1912.

SIR DANIELS

The original SIR DANIELS were a class of 30 GWR single-wheelers which were built to Joseph Armstrong's order in 1866-69. These singles differed from those of his predecessor, Daniel Gooch, by having double frames of solid plate. Four were named, and one carried the name *Sir Daniel*. By the end of the century loads had grown too heavy for the old singles, and, after scrapping three, William Dean embarked on the rather startling course of rebuilding the remainder into 0-6-0 goods engines. Churchward stopped the process when he took over in 1902; thus, four unaltered singles died a natural death in 1904.

One can imagine the sensation F.W. Webb created when his first long-boilered compound 2-2-2-2s emerged from Crewe Works in 1891-94. No 527 *Henry Bessemer* (Works No 3476/1894), like the others, did not live long to relish, or otherwise, its nicknames SHOOTING GALLERY and LONG STOMACH, for it was cut up in January 1907. *Author's Collection*

Meanwhile, the so-called SIR DANIEL 0-6-0s did not last much longer. Most vanished in the 1900s, and only one specimen, No 381, lingered on until December 1919.

SKITTLE ALLEYS
Again, this nickname was a reflection on boiler length, and was applied to two enormous 'Pacifics' which were produced by Sir Vincent Raven for the NER on the eve of the Grouping. Three more emerged from Darlington Works in 1924. Presumably intended as a bid to secure NER design for future LNER express locomotive requirements, the 'Cities', as they were known, failed to prevent the wholesale adoption of Gresley's rival GNR 'Pacific' design. Efforts were made in due course by the LNER to render the SKITTLE ALLEYS satisfactory, but the inescapable fact remained that Raven had produced an elongated 'Atlantic', while Gresley had designed a completely new

'Pacific'. Accordingly, all five SKITTLE ALLEYS succumbed in 1936-37.

SKYE BOGIES
This popular nickname was applied to a hardy new class of o/c 4-4-0 which was introduced by the HR to supplement those already working on its Skye line, with all its attendant difficulties. Though designed by David Jones, the SKYE BOGIES followed accepted Allan lines, but were given 5 ft 3 in coupled wheels to meet Skye line requirements. The first was built at Lochgorm Works in 1882, and only after a 10-year lapse were four more added. Peter Drummond contributed another four in 1897-1901. Seven reached the Grouping, and the last pair, Jones No 14277 and Drummond No 14284, were withdrawn in June 1930. See also MARY.

SMALL BLOOMERS
See BLOOMERS.

Sheer length of boiler was also enough to earn ex-NER 4-6-2 No 2402 *City of York* and her four sisters the nickname SKITTLE ALLEYS. No 2402, in fact, had the ultimate melancholy distinction of being the first LNER-built locomotive to be scrapped—in July 1936. *Author's Collection*

SMALL BOGIES

Six 'new design' i/c 4-4-0s were built by Sharp Stewart for the Cambrian Railways in 1878-91, and later, when larger engines were introduced, the Sharps became known as SMALL BOGIES. The first two bore names, but these were removed by December 1891. Smart-looking locomotives, they coped admirably with summer traffic, until the LARGE BOGIES were introduced in 1893. Sixteen of the latter were built by Sharp Stewart, R. Stephenson & Co added four more in 1897-98, and Oswestry Works produced a final pair in 1901-04. All of the BOGIES, SMALL and LARGE, passed into GWR ownership, and the last SMALL BOGIE, No 1118, was not withdrawn until October 1930. Surprisingly, the LARGE BOGIES had perished almost to a man by that time, and one survivor, renumbered 1110 in 1926, was placed on the Sales List in 1931.

SMALL HAWTHORNS

Twenty of these 2-2-2s, ordered by Benjamin Cubitt, were supplied to the GNR by R.&W. Hawthorn & Co in 1848-50, and six were lent to the East Kent Railway Co, later the LC&DR, in 1860 (see GEORDIES). Two of the GNR SMALL HAWTHORNS were later converted to 0-4-2s, with 6-foot driving wheels, by Patrick Stirling.

Hawthorn also provided the GNR with 12 LARGE HAWTHORN 2-2-2s in 1852-53. Most were later rebuilt, and only two reached 1890.

SMALL HOPPERS

See GRASSHOPPERS.

SMALL WHEELED FISH

A Manchester area nickname for the LNER (ex-GCR) Class 'B9' 4-6-0s (see FISH).

THE SNATCHER

The Isle of Wight Central Railway's locomotive No 3, a neat little Black Hawthorn 0-4-2ST known first as *Mill Hill*, had an inauspicious start to its career, when a barge conveying it from the mainland listed during unloading, and deposited the little engine in the sea. Nevertheless, No 3 entered traffic on 24 March 1870. In later years, when it was relegated to shunting duties at Medina Wharf, the saddle tank came to be known locally as THE SNATCHER; one presumes that the nickname was a reflection of its loin-girding habits when 'taking the strain'. A new firebox was fitted in 1904, and in 1909 No 3 was converted to railmotor use at Newport Works, at a cost of £437. On 30 October 1917 the IWCR advertised the little 0-4-2ST for sale, and it and No 4 went to Holloway Bros Ltd, London, for £1,700. It was finally broken up at Haverton Hill early in 1920.

THE SOJER

Far north of the Border, GNSR men did not appear to invent locomotive nicknames readily, and it was probably members of the public who nicknamed No 49 *Gordon Highlander*, one of six lovely Class 'F' i/c 4-4-0s which were built by NBL in 1920 to the requirements of T.E. Heywood. Working constantly in a locality which maintained 'ye're nae a sojer if ye're nae a Gordon', the engine inevitably acquired the nickname THE SOJER. Numbered 62277 under BR auspices, THE SOJER outlived the others of its class, and, officially withdrawn in June 1958, is now preserved in the Glasgow Transport Museum.

SOUTH LONDON TANKS

These were a series of unusually diverse 0-4-2WTs which were designed by J.C. Craven to handle LB&SCR South London line suburban traffic. The first two, built at Brighton in 1865, were symptomatic of Craven's inbuilt aversion to standardisation, for one appeared with inside frames and bearings, and the other with double frames and outside bearings! Again, of six more added in 1866, two were well tanks, while the remainder were turned out as side tanks at a cost of £1,994 each. Generally speaking, the performance of Craven's SOUTH LONDON TANKS lacked distinction, and services improved vastly when Stroudley's 'D1' and TERRIER (qv) tanks took over. By 1886 the last was seen of Craven's odd miscellany.

SPACE SHIPS

Where BR-designed 2-10-0s were concerned, the clear view one could obtain between boiler and wheels led some enthusiasts to refer to these locomotives as SPACE SHIPS. But see also COMBINE HARVESTERS.

SPAM CANS

This rather unkind nickname was applied to O.V.S. Bulleid's 'Merchant Navy' 'Pacifics' of 1941. 'Spam' in cans was already a familiar part of the nation's wartime diet, and the temptation to link the term with these remarkable new SR engines, with their air-smoothed exterior, was irresistible. In the event, the class was extended to 30 in post-war years, and, of course, a similar form of streamlining obtained when Bulleid's 'West Country' and 'Battle of Britain' 'Pacifics' followed in 1945-46. The final tally of SPAM CANS built between 1941 and 1951 amounted to 140. Many were rebuilt in unstreamlined form between 1956 and 1961, and final withdrawal of the class was effected by July 1967. No 35029 *Ellerman Lines* is now a sectioned exhibit at the National Railway Museum, York, and quite a number of other Bulleid 'Pacifics' have been preserved throughout the UK.

Presumably as a Cockney rhyming slang play on the name *Channel Packet*, that of the prototype engine, 'Merchant Navy' locomotives were also known, particularly in the London area, as FLANNEL JACKETS.

SPAM CARS

These were a final series of noticeably smaller GWR 0-6-0 pannier tanks, built in 1949-55 and usefully employed by BR on Western Region routes with low overbridges. Built to a restricted loading gauge, the tanks had a compact appearance which, coupled to wartime memories of 'Spam' and other imported delicacies, inspired the nickname SPAM CARS—particularly when the tanks were used on branch auto-trains. One, No 1638, has survived to find employment on the Dart Valley Railway.

Seen here as built in 1941, the startling appearance of SR No 21C1 indicates quite clearly why the class became known as SPAM CANS. Presumably the name of the prototype engine, *Channel Packet*, gave rise to a second nickname, FLANNEL JACKETS. *Steamchest*

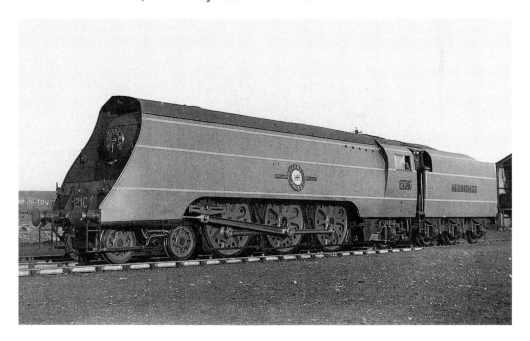

SPANKERS/SPANKING ENGINES

When R.C. Sinclair moved from the CR to the ECR in 1856, his first design for the latter produced six 2-4-0 goods engines which bore a marked similarity to CR practice. His next locomotives, however, a series of Class 'Y' express goods 2-4-0s, broke away from the Caledonian tradition of outside frames and inclined o/cs. The first 20, built by Neilson & Co in 1859-60, featured a dome over the firebox, and carried the usual weatherboard behind. Ninety more, supplied by various makers, including Scheider et Cie of Creusot, had the dome plumb in the centre of the boiler, and introduced vastly improved cabs. Extremely handsome and versatile engines, their stovepipe chimneys added a further rakish element, Known as SPANKERS, or SPANKING ENGINES, by ECR men, many were rebuilt by the GER, and the last survivor went in December 1894.

SPECIAL DX

See DXs.

SPINNERS

The invention at Derby Works of an apparatus which sanded rails by steam, instead of gravity, prompted the MR to resuscitate the single-wheeler for main-line express work. Thus, four very beautiful 4-2-2s emerged from Derby between the years 1887 and 1889; 85 were ultimately constructed, and 43 reached the Grouping, though they perished within five years. The last batch of 15 boasted of 7 ft 9½ in driving wheels, and, even with the sanding apparatus, they displayed a capacity for slipping which earned them the nickname SPINNERS. The last in service of that series was preserved at Derby in MR livery as No 118 after withdrawal in April 1928. It now appears in public, how-ever, bearing its later number, 673.

SPINNING JENNIES

For the opening of its Andover line, the Swindon, Marlborough & Andover Railway, later absorbed by the M&SWJR, bought three standard Beyer Peacock 2-4-0Ts in 1883, at a cost of £1,993 10s 11d each. With polished dome, tall copper-capped chimney, low-roofed cab, and an absence of angle irons around the footplate, the little tanks were similar to those which had been supplied to the Dutch State Railways in 1877-78. Numbered 5-7, they served the M&SWJR well, and, highly popular engines, they were known as SPINNING JENNIES. No 6 went to the Isle of Wight Central Railway for £700 in 1906, and No 7, the last survivor, was broken up in 1910. A fourth SPINNING JENNY, No 8, supplied by Beyer Peacock in 1884, was sold in January 1918.

THE SPOUT

This apt nickname was bestowed upon ex-LMSR Ivatt MT 2-6-0 No 43027 when it was experimentally fitted with a very narrow stovepipe chimney. A lip, subsequently fitted to the chimney, improved the locomotive's appearance slightly, but the last-built of the class reverted once more to the standard wide chimney. All 162 of this numerous class served well into the 1960s.

SQUARE BELLIES

A none too complementary, but self-explanatory, nickname which was applied to GWR 0-6-0 pannier tanks as a species.

SQUAREBOXES

These were two extraordinary o/c 0-4-0Ts which, reputedly built by Neilson & Co of Glasgow in 1854, were employed on the Goosemoor section of the West Somerset Mineral Railway. The boiler of these 13-ton locomotives was surrounded, back and front, by a large boxlike tank, the front of which was flush with the smokebox; a stovepipe chimney and dumb wooden buffers completed a totally bizarre effect. The fate of these engines is not known.

SQUARE CABS

James Stirling's final design for the SER before his retirement in 1898 resulted in 29 extremely handsome Class 'B' i/c 4-4-0s being built. Neilson Reid & Co supplied 20 between July and September 1898, and Ashford Works added nine more between Octo-

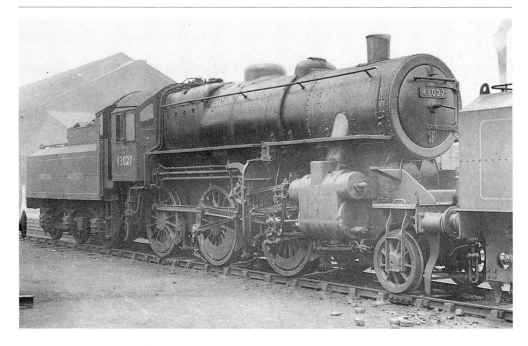

One can see from this Willesden shed picture of Ivatt MT '4F' 2-6-0 No 43027 why the engine soon acquired the nickname THE SPOUT. *Author*

ber 1898 and July 1899. Basically these engines were similar to Stirling's earlier JUMBOS (qv), but they had larger boilers, shorter chimneys and wider tenders; it was their new type of square cab which gave them their nickname, All but two, rebuilt later with domed boilers, were reclassified 'B1'. But even in SR days they were still known to loco men as STIRLINGS.

STANDARD GOODS
Joseph Armstrong developed a class of double-framed Standard Goods 0-6-0s from 1866 onwards, at a time when the GWR badly needed a uniform type to replace the miscellaneous classes it had inherited from various amalgamations. In the event a total of 250 STANDARD GOODS emerged from Swindon between 1866 and 1876, and as the class grew in number it became customary for GWR men to refer to the older 0-6-0s as ARMSTRONG GOODS. Meanwhile, Armstrong's hardy new 0-6-0s tackled all kinds of work. Quite a number served overseas under ROD auspices during the First World War,

though not all returned. Most achieved one million miles during their lifetime and the last, No 1195, hung on to October 1934.

The GNR, too, was very partial to employing 0-6-0 goods engines, and, of the 393 it handed over to the LNER at the Grouping, 228 were of one basic pattern of STANDARD GOODS. Patrick Stirling introduced the type in 1873, and H.A. Ivatt continued to develop them. Even Gresley added to their ranks before he blossomed in other directions. Tough, reliable locomotives, they led very busy lives indeed, and 41 of them, by then LNER Classes 'J3' and 'J4', entered BR stock; the last seven were withdrawn in 1953-54. Earlier in life, the GNR STANDARD GOODS were also known as 'B' ENGINES, because of their load classification.

STANDARDS
See UKELELES.

STEAM BOATS
These were six 0-6-0STs which were supplied by Neilson & Co to the CR in 1881.

GWR 0-6-0 No 610, built at Swindon in 1871 (Works No 298), was a member of Joseph Armstrong's prolific STANDARD GOODS class. Seen here as built, No 610, though never superheated, experienced two boiler changes before the breakers claimed it in May 1921. *Author's Collection*

Equipped with a vertical hand brake and employed solely on shunting duties, they became known as STEAM BOATS in the River Clyde area. Only one survived to enter LMSR stock; as No 16150 it was withdrawn in 1928.

STEAM BRAKERS

The only goods engines designed by Hugh Smellie for the G&SWR, his 0-6-0s were first shopped from Kilmarnock Works in 1881-82, and the class grew to 64 by 1892 as Neilson & Co and Dubs added their quotas. Originally domeless, some were later given domes by James Manson. Meanwhile, they were the first G&SWR engines to be fitted with the steam brake, and, as such, they were known to Sou' Western men as the STEAM BRAKERS. Quite a number entered LMSR stock in rebuilt form, and two even lasted until 1927.

STEAM ROLLERS

In 1879 Beyer Peacock & Co supplied the LSWR with 12 Adams-designed '380' Class 4-4-0 MT locomotives at a cost of £2,540 each. With roomy square cabs, solid bogie wheels and stovepipe chimneys, they soon acquired the nickname STEAM ROLLERS, more appropriately than ever in view of the noise they made when running light. For a number of years the handling of a variety of passenger and goods workings all over the West of England fell to their lot. Later a number were transferred to Strawberry Hill shed, whence they worked freight trains from Battersea Yard, and across London to the MR sidings at Brent. The Battersea connection was enough to earn them the additional nickname of DOG'S HOME SHUNTERS. By 1902 Dugald Drummond's new 'K10' 4-4-0s took over mixed traffic duties from the '380s', and all the latter entered the LSWR's

Duplicate List. Remarkably, most worked on into the early 1920s, and the last pair were not withdrawn until December 1925.

STELLAS

During 1884-87 William Dean carried out a standardisation programme on the GWR which involved four classes of engine— passenger tender and tank, and goods tender and tank. First of a series, No 3201, a 2-4-0 tender locomotive, was sold as new to the Pembroke & Tenby Railway before any others were built. By the time the engine returned to the GWR fold in 1896 it bore the name *Stella*, and under GWR auspices it continued to carry the name until 1902. Although none of the remaining standardised GWR 2-4-0 class ever carried names, the class itself inevitably became known as the STELLAS. No 3201, nameless latterly, was the last to go, in October 1933.

STIRLINGS

See SQUARE CABS.

STONES

When, after gaining a through route to Doncaster in 1892, the GER found itself faced with a considerable volume of newly acquired goods traffic, T.W. Worsdell solved the problem by initiating production of the most numerous locomotive class the GER ever owned, his hugely popular 'Y14' Class, of which a total of 289 were built between 1883 and 1913. Such was Stratford Works' efficency at the time, that Crewe Works' record of 25½ hours was completely eclipsed in December 1891 when 'Y14' No 930 was erected and put in steam in the astonishing time of 9 hours 47 minutes (see COAL ENGINES). The locomotive itself was withdrawn on 31 January 1936, with 1,127,750 miles to its credit, but 125 of the class survived to enter BR stock in 1948. In their heyday the 'Y14s', latterly LNER Class 'J15', cheerfully handled any traffic that came their way. GER men referred to them as STONES, but the origin of that nickname remains obscure. Fittingly, No 65462, withdrawn from Stratford shed in September 1962, has been preserved by the North Norfolk Railway.

STRAIGHTBACKS

Patrick Stirling held firmly to the view that locomotive boilers did not require domes. His younger brother, James, followed the same philosophy on the G&SWR and SER, and family tradition was faithfully consolidated on the H&BR by Patrick's son, Matthew. All the latter's locomotive designs were inside-cylindered, and, being domeless to boot, were soon known as STRAIGHTBACKS. Latterly, those which survived the Grouping were fitted with domed boilers by the LNER.

A class of 34 domeless 2-4-0s which were introduced on the L&YR by William Hurst in 1870-76 were also known as STRAIGHTBACKS.

STREAKS

Gresley's streamlined Class 'A4' 'Pacifics', 35 of which were built by the LNER in 1935-38, aroused enormous interest, both public and professional, particularly when, on 27 September 1935, No 2509 *Silver Link* notched a maximum speed of 112½ mph when hauling a seven-coach 'Silver Jubilee' express on a trial run between King's Cross and Grantham. LNER men's pride was even further enhanced on 3 July 1938, when No 4468 *Mallard* established a new world record for steam, by sustaining a speed of 126 mph for all of 5 miles, again with a seven-coach train. Thus one nickname for the class, the STREAKS, was well earned. Six of these remarkable engines have been preserved, including, of course, the immortal *Mallard*.

STRETCHER

This old six-coupled engine, built *circa* 1900 at Chesterfield, was employed by Powesland & Mason, the contractors who handled traffic at Swansea Harbour, until the Swansea Harbour Trust was absorbed by the GWR in July 1923. The STRETCHER was so called because of its long stovepipe chimney, and appears to have been sold to a Swansea scrap merchant in 1913.

STRAIGHTBACKS. During his long career with the H&BR, Matthew Stirling followed his father's philosophy by building only domeless engines. Now LNER Class 'J23', No 2517 was built by Kitson & Co (Works No 136/1908) as H&BR No 136. Later numbered 3137 by the NER, then given No 2517 by the LNER, the loco was withdrawn in July 1937. *G.R. Grigs*

STUPID Ds

F.W. Webb introduced his first eight-coupled LNWR freight engine in 1892, and from this a much-loved line of 572 0-8-0s was generated over the years to 1922. All but one, No 134, which exploded at Buxton on 11 November 1921, lasted into the LMSR era. Webb's first big class, the 'As', consisted of 111 engines, built between 1893 and 1900. His successor, George Whale, rebuilt 63 of them from 3-cyl compound to 2-cyl simple in 1906-09. Now known as Class 'D', they had a distinct characteristic of emitting steam and strange noises from odd places, and, quite affectionately, they were nicknamed variously by LNWR men STUPID Ds, CHOO CHOOS and MOURNERS. Just the same, all 63 contrived to enter BR stock, albeit in rebuilt form, in 1948. See also FAT NANCIES.

SUBMARINES

See ARDSLEY TANKS.

SUPER CLAUDS

See CLAUDS.

SUPER Ds

See FAT NANCIES and STUPID Ds.

SUPERHEATED WET STEAMERS

See WET STEAMERS.

SWALLOWTAILS

When six Stephenson Patent long boilered passenger singles were ordered from Jones & Potts by the Brighton, Croydon & Dover Joint Committee in 1844, all were delivered after the Committee had been dissolved. As a consequence, two of the Jones & Potts engines, Nos 117 and 118, went to the SER. There they soon proved to be unsteady riders at speeds of 30-35 mph, and both were subsequently rebuilt as 2-2-2 well tanks, for employment on the Greenwich line. Known there as SWALLOWTAILS, both little locomotives were laid aside in 1859.

SWAMIES

Nearly 40 4-cyl compound 2-8-0s were built by the LNWR in 1901. Controversial engines, they appear to have attracted the nickname SWAMIES via the notorious criminals, Theo and Swami, whose prosecution attracted much public attention that year. An alternative school of thought maintains that the nickname reflected the capacity of these compounds to swamp themselves in steam from leaky joints. In some LNWR areas, 0-8-0s, too, were regarded as SWAMIES. Whatever, soon after the Grouping all surviving LNWR compounds were converted to Class 'G1' 0-8-0s, and, of these, the last rebuild lasted until 1964. See also PIANO FRONTS.

The large-boilered 4-cyl compound 2-8-0s which were introduced by Whale in 1904-07 were, inevitably, dubbed BIG SWAMIES.

SWEAT BOXES

See CHIP VANS.

SWEDES

This was the GNR and GCR men's nickname for GER engines in general.

SWIFTS

The Class 'N31' 0-6-0s, later LNER 'J14', were designed by James Holden in a bid to achieve a greater measure of standardisation in GER locomotive practice, but although 81 were built at Stratford Works during 1893-98, they were not a success. Indeed, GER men referred to them sardonically as SWIFTS because of their sluggishness. Scrapping commenced in 1908, and the LNER only inherited 17 of the original engines. Even those were withdrawn over the years 1923-25. See also WATERBURIES.

T

TAFFIES

LNWR locomotives were frequently known as TAFFIES in the Nottingham area.

TAILWAGGERS

See LITTLE SHARPIES.

TAMBOURINIES

H.A. Ivatt's last design for the GNR before he retired in December 1911 saw 15 'D1' class 4-4-0s shopped from Doncaster Works that year. Once the GNR's 'Atlantics' assumed full main-line command, however, the 'D1s' were relegated to lesser duties, and in 1925 the LNER shipped all 15 to Scotland, ostensibly to relieve a locomotive shortage there. NBR men were normally quite adept at adjusting themselves to handling 'foreign' engines, but in this instance the 'D1s' gained immediate, and extreme, unpopularity. They were rough riders, and Scottish locomen disliked their draughty cabs and footplate fittings. Even when fitted with Westinghouse pumps, the 'D1s' were confined to very minor duties, and were dubbed PONIES and TAMBOURINIES. Seven of them were returned to the Southern Area in 1930-32 on an expected exchange basis for seven ex-GNR 'D3s', although the latter were sent, instead, to the NE Area. In the event, seven 'D1s' entered BR service, with five of them still in Scotland. But it was a Norwich engine which last met the breakers, when No 62209 was scrapped in November 1950.

TANGOS

The GNR's Class 'O2' 2-8-0s, 11 in number and introduced by Gresley in 1918, were popular and hard-working engines, so much so that a further 56 were built after the Grouping. Three-cylindered, the locomotive's motion produced a distinctive Gresley 'clank', and that, plus a tendency to settle down on their springs and a rather sinuous gait once they got going, earned them the nickname TANGOS, after the dance which became so popular in the mid-1920s. All except the prototype engine danced their way into the early 1960s—and the last five did not leave the floor until November 1963.

TAR TANKS

See BUCK JUMPERS.

TATER ROASTERS

This self-explanatory nickname was heart-feltly bestowed by locomen who knew, and suffered in, the cabs of the LNWR's quite numerous 0-4-2 and 0-6-0 shunting tanks!

TEDDY BEARS

See BULLDOGS.

TENNANTS

In 1895 the NER introduced a non-stop run from Newcastle to Edinburgh, but badly required suitable new engines. The NER's Locomotive Superintendent, A. McDonnell, having resigned, a Committee was formed by the General Manager, H. Tennant, and they produced a 7-foot 2-4-0, known thereafter as the TENNANT class. All 20 built became Class 'E5' on the LNER, and No 1474, the last to be withdrawn, went in February 1929. Earlier, No 1463 took part in the Stockton & Darlington Centenary procession of 1925. Fortunately, when the locomotive was condemned in August 1927 it was repainted in NER livery, and placed in the LNER's York Railway Museum.

TERRIERS

During his years with the LB&SCR William Stroudley designed many elegant engines, but none earned greater fame than the diminutive 0-6-0Ts he introduced in 1872. Before long, the tenacious approach of these little tanks to whatever task they were offered earned them the affectionate nickname of TERRIERS, which term first appeared in *The Engineer* of February 1873. The locomotives were also known as ROOTERS and PUPS by some of their crews, but the term TERRIER has best stood the test of time, and, astonishingly, 10 still survive to tell the tale.

THUMPER

This was a clumsy looking 0-6-0ST which was purchased by the SE&CR from a contractor, William Rigby, for £400 in 1904. The locomotive was built by Manning Wardle in 1879, and, despite her age and appearance,

A rare example of a locomotive designed by a Committee, NER TENNANT No 1464 was built at Darlington in 1885; for their first 10 years these gallant 2-4-0s each averaged over 40,000 miles per annum on main-line duties. Superceded latterly by 4-4-0s, they gradually relinquished first-class passenger work, and No 1464 was withdrawn from Kirkby Stephen shed in February 1929. *Steamchest*

was given full SE&CR green livery once she reported to Ashford Works. First employed at Folkestone Harbour, the 0-6-0 tank was sent to Kent during the First World War, and there, because of the noise she generated at speeds above 5 mph, she was nicknamed THUMPER. After the Grouping, the Manning Wardle loco was transferred to Dover, then, in August 1925, she was laid aside at Ashford, and was sold to George Cohen & Co in March 1926 for £250.

TILBURY UNIVERSAL MACHINES

Incorporated as a separate company in 1862, the LT&SR was worked until 3 July 1880 by locomotives which were provided by the Eastern Counties Railway and the GER. An intensive suburban passenger requirement east of Fenchurch Street station soon revealed itself, and in 1880 William Adams of the GER supervised the design of a suitable locomotive to handle the LT&SR's burgeoning traffic. The result was the classic TILBURY UNIVERSAL MACHINE, an o/c 4-4-2T. Thirty of these graceful tanks were supplied by Sharp Stewart in 1880-84, and Nasmyth Wilson & Co built six more in 1892. So successful was the class that three more batches, by various makers, followed over the years 1897-1909, and all bore the names of local towns and villages. In 1923 the LMSR, unable to furnish a more suitable type, built 10 more, and added a further 25 during 1925-30, after which Stanier provided a capable 2-6-4T substitute. The last TILBURY UNIVERSAL MACHINE to survive, LMS-built No 41947, was withdrawn in November 1960; fortunately, No 80 *Thundersley*, a 1909 veteran, was preserved, and can presently be seen at the Bressingham Railway Museum. See also THE CAMEL.

TIN CANS

This nickname was rather unjustly conferred on William Pickersgill's CR Class '3F' 0-6-0s, 43 of which were built at St Rollox Works in 1918-20. The first dozen were obliged by Ministry regulations to have steel fireboxes, and in general these engines were not so robustly built as the Drummond and McIntosh 0-6-0s which preceded them. December 1963 saw the last of the TIN CANS, when No 57688 was withdrawn.

TINIES

This affectionate appreciation was coined by L&YR men when J.A.F. Aspinall's massive Class 'L1' 'Atlantics' made their debut in 1899. The largest British express engines of their time, the 40 'L1s' had 7 ft 3 in driving wheels, and a high-pitched boiler added to their impressive demeanour. The last, No 10316, was withdrawn in March 1934. See also HIGHFLYERS.

The nickname TINIES was equally cheerfully bestowed by GCR men on J.G. Robinson's 2-8-0s (see RODs) and 0-8-0s (see OLD LADIES).

TIN LIZZIES

See RAGTIMERS and RODs.

TISHIES

In 1923, under the supervision of H.P.M. Beames, the LNWR's CME, four 'Prince of Wales' 4-6-0s and one new engine of the same type were fitted with Walschaerts valve motion *outside* the frame. The object was to eliminate the hole in the connecting rod from which the valve drive was taken in locomotives fitted with Joy's motion, to thus minimise the likelihood of bent rods when valve friction became excessive. The odd visual effect of the crossed rods of the Walschaerts motion resulted in the first of these engines being nicknamed TISHY, after a well-known racehorse which vexed owners and punters alike by crossing its forelegs when running—then falling! The newly built 'Prince', supplied by W. Beardmore & Co in May 1924, was later numbered LMSR 5845. Whilst on show at the Wembley Exhibition that year the name *Prince of Wales* was added. New nameplates, however, were provided—*not* those off No 5600.

TODS

This was a trio of 0-4-0s which, built by Bury Curtis & Kennedy, were purchased second-

One of five LNWR TISHIES, No 964 was duly fitted with external Walschaerts valve gear in March 1923. Shopped from Crewe (Works No 5189) in February 1914, and involved in an accident at Ardwick, Manchester, on 19 July 1929, *Bret Harte* was withdrawn in 1933. *Author's Collection*

hand by the Dundee & Perth & Aberdeen Junction Railway in 1854. There, for some unknown reason, they were given the nickname TODS, a Scottish word for foxes. The DPAJR duly amalgamated with the Scottish Central Railway on 28 July 1863, and the 'foxes' were scrapped very shortly after receiving SCR Nos 63-65.

TOGOS
Here we have L&YR men's fanciful nickname for 20 large i/c 2-6-2Ts which were built at Horwich in 1903-04 to the order of H.A. Hoy. With a water capacity of 2,000 gallons and a bunker capable of holding $3\frac{3}{4}$ tons of coal, these tanks were designed to handle local passenger work on steeply-graded lines around Manchester. Their long rigid coupled wheelbase, however, tended to spread the track, and, of course, this made the tanks unpopular. In 1908 the central coupled wheels were made flangeless, but by 1914 the class had lost its local passenger work to much smaller superheated L&YR 2-4-2Ts, and

thereafter the 2-6-2Ts reverted to shunting duties. Most passed into LMSR ownership, but the last of the class vanished in August 1926. These large L&YR tanks had a very sleek appearance, and possibly the nickname implied a similarity to Admiral Togo, a belligerent Japanese Navy admiral of the time.

TOMATO HOUSES
See CRYSTAL PALACES.

TOWN HALLS
This nickname was lavished by LSWR men on William Adams's 4-4-0s, at all times superbly built and utterly reliable locomotives. The term also implied the element of quality which hallmarked Adams's contribution to LSWR locomotive practice in general, particularly after W.G. Beattie's disastrous term of office. Adams rebuilt so many 'old crocks', and introduced so many new types, including eight classes of 4-4-0, that his successor in office, Dugald Drummond, had few immediate locomotive problems to face.

Those which arose later were largely of Drummond's own making!

TRAMS

The GER used 0-4-0 steam tram locomotives as far back as 1883, for use alongside public highways at Wisbech and Yarmouth. Then, in 1903, James Holden designed a more powerful 0-6-0 version, with o/cs and Walschaerts valve gear, of which 12 were ultimately constructed at Stratford Works. Because their design had to comply with Board of Trade regulations, these TRAMS were fitted with cowcatcher, warning bell, protective skirting over the wheels, and governors which limited speed to 8 mph. They spent a lifetime working in East Anglia, and the first pair, built in 1903, lasted 50 years. The LNER classified them 'J70' and, like the earlier 0-4-0 trams, by then LNER Class 'Y6', which were toughly built, the upper part of the 'J70' was enclosed by a wooden body which closely resembled a traditional goods brake van.

No 68083, the last of the 11 'Y6' trams, was withdrawn in November 1952; an intention to preserve the locomotive was never implemented. Most of the dozen 'J70' trams worked on into the 1950s, the last four being condemned in 1955.

TRAWLERS

These were a group of five 0-6-2Ts which were built by Kitson & Co in 1900 to the order of the LD&ECR. The order was later cancelled owing to lack of funds, and the H&BR bought all five from Kitson in 1901. Later classified by the LNER as 'N11', the tanks were known as TRAWLERS in the Hull locality because of a similarity in whistle sound to that of fishing boats in the harbour. All were withdrawn in the mid-1940s.

TUNNEL MOTORS

By 1933 the GWR 2-4-0 and 0-6-0Ts which, carrying condensing gear, traditionally worked the Metropolitan Railway lines to

Photographed at Old Oak Common on 17 June 1962, ex-GWR TUNNEL MOTOR No 9710 displays the condensing equipment, ATC gear and extended water tanks which made the class eminently suitable for working over Metropolitan lines to Smithfield. *Author*

Smithfield, London, were falling due for replacement. After initial experiment with 0-6-0PT No 8700, Swindon then shopped 10 new pannier tanks. These were equipped with special ATC apparatus which automatically cleared live rails on entering an electrified section, and was released again on leaving it. No 8700 was renumbered 9700 in January 1934, to complete the class (Nos 9700-10). With their frequent employment on freight trains through the 'Met' tunnels, mainly at night, they soon became known as the TUNNEL MOTORS.

TURBOMOTIVE

When W.A. Stanier, CME to the LMSR, visited Sweden in the early 1930s at the invitation of Metro-Vickers he was greatly impressed by the working of a new Ljungstrom turbine 2-8-0 locomotive. As a consequence it was decided that the LMSR's third 'Pacific' should be built on similar principles. Thus Crewe Works shopped, in July 1935, what appeared to be an i/c version of its 'Princess Royal' Class. In fact, it employed two non-condensing turbines, one for forward motion, one for reverse. Results on test were encouraging; the TURBOMOTIVE, as it was unofficially christened, ran smoothly, without slip or hammer blow, and it was utilised frequently on London–Liverpool express work right up to the outbreak of war in 1939. Unfortunately specialist maintenance problems required No 6202 to be stored at Crewe over the war years. Once hostilities ceased, however, it ran again—until 1952, when the TURBOMOTIVE was converted to a conventional reciprocating locomotive, and named *Princess Anne*. Life after that was only too short, for the engine was completely wrecked in the Harrow railway disaster of 8 October that year.

THE TURKEY

Dugald Drummond was not a man who was easily deflected, particularly from his self-appointed mission of providing the LSWR with six-coupled express locomotives. His first five 4-6-0s, Class 'F13', built in 1905, were a gross disappointment, and, reacting

LMSR TURBOMOTIVE No 6202 looks comfortable enough heading the 'Merseyside Express'. Unfortunately, this advanced locomotive only achieved an average annual mileage of 28,500 in this form, before being converted to conventional 'Princess Royal' style in 1952. *Author's Collection*

cautiously, he confined his next six-coupled venture to one engine, even though his Locomotive Committee had, in fact, sanctioned the construction of five. Thus in November 1907, No 335, the sole representative of Class 'E14', emerged from Nine Elms Works.

Again, the long shallow firebox Drummond persisted in fitting proved ineffectual, and on test, with *two* firemen on board, a coal consumption of 50¾ lbs per mile soon revealed No 335's inadequacy for express work. Even when the locomotive was relegated to main-line goods duties, her voracious appetite for coal did not lessen. Thus, on the Southampton–Nine Elms goods run she soon acquired notoriety as THE TURKEY. No one, it seemed, could reduce her enormous appetite. Latterly, in the interest of leaving the fireman fresh for his herculean task *en route*, the practice was adopted of seeing that No 335's coal supply was broken up *before* she left the shed! The engine was, in fact, withdrawn in June 1914, after running only 112,405 miles. Robert Urie, however, salvaged parts from her to add one more to his infinitely more successful 2-cyl 'H15' Class of 4-6-0. With this new lease of life, remnants of THE TURKEY lasted until June 1959.

THE TWELVE APOSTLES

When Hugh Smellie prepared his first design for the G&SWR, he chose, rather suprisingly in the year 1879, to build 12 2-4-0 tender engines, which were shopped from Kilmarnock Works in two batches. The total weight was 38½ tons, and their coupled wheels of 6 ft 9½ in set G&SWR express locomotive standards for 25 years to follow. The 2-4-0s proved to be an immediate success, and their popularity with G&SWR men can be gauged by the nickname they earned—THE TWELVE APOSTLES. Nos 14001/02 survived to limp into LMSR stock in 1923, but both vanished that year.

Hugh Smellie's first design for the G&SWR, 2-4-0 No 185 was one of his immortal TWELVE APOSTLES. Shopped at Kilmarnock (Works No 146) in December 1879, this engine was Duplicate Listed as 185A in July 1909, and went to the breakers in 1912. *Author's Collection*

U

U BOATS

The SR's first 20 'U' Class 2-6-0s were, because of their graphic pedigree, known by train crews as 'REBUILT RIVERS' (qv). Thirty more, built at Ashford and Brighton Works in 1928-31, being completely new engines, were accepted without equivocation as U BOATS. Highly popular and versatile locomotives, all Class 'U' 2-6-0s, regardless of pedigree, lasted well into the 1960s, and four which have been preserved offer an interesting selection. No 31806, owned by the Mid Hants Railway, was formerly 'K' tank *River Torridge*. Their other 'U', No 31625, was built at Ashford in 1929. Conversely, one of the Bluebell Railway's Class 'Us', withdrawn from Guildford shed in 1964 as BR No 31618, was originally being assembled as a Class 'K' 2-6-4T—until repercussions of the Sevenoaks disaster (see REBUILT RIVERS) stopped all further production. Otherwise the engine might well have borne the name *River Hamble*, instead of being completed as Class 'U' 2-6-0 No 1618 at Brighton Works in October 1928. The Bluebell's second 'U', No 31638, was, on the other hand, one of a final 10 which were shopped from Ashford Works in May 1929.

UKELELES

This numerous class of 5 ft 2 in 'J39' 0-6-0 was introduced on the LNER by Gresley in 1926. By 1941 a total of 289 had been built, making the 'J39s' Gresley's most prolific class. Known in the West Riding district and GCR Section as STANDARDS, they were dubbed elsewhere, less respectfully, as UKELELES. The 'J39s', however, were recognised as a powerful and versatile addition to LNER stock, and could handle freight and passenger trains with equal nonchalance. All were withdrawn between 1959 and 1962, and, alas, no specimen remains in captivity.

USA TANKS

These were 14 0-6-0Ts which the SR purchased, in 1946, from the American War Department at £2,500 apiece, mainly for work in Southampton Docks. Despite their distinctly American appearance, they were popular with enginemen around the Docks, though various modification had to be effected as minor problems revealed themselves. Compared to their predecessors, the ex-LSWR 'B4' 0-4-0Ts, the US tanks' active life in dockland was short, for the advent of diesel locomotives in 1962 soon led to their retirement. Sundry minor duties elsewhere followed, but by September 1967 the whole class was withdrawn. Two, Nos 30064 and 30072, were rescued from the breakers by the Bluebell and Keighley & Worth Valley railways respectively. The Kent & East Sussex Railway also owns two, which are now styled No 21 *Wainwright* and No 22 *Maunsell*.

UTILITIES

A familiar phrase during the Second World War, this nickname was applied to the SR's new radically designed 'Q1' Class 0-6-0s of 1942. So, too, were the even less charitable nicknames of WARTHOGS and CHARLIES. Wartime restrictions made it necessary to abandon many conventional features of locomotive design when the 'Q1s' were built at Ashford and Brighton Works. The public were, accordingly, somewhat startled in 1942 to find 40 locomotives in their midst with large diameter stovepipe chimneys and squarish gaunt-looking sectional boilers. Gone was the sleek cladded shell they knew so well! Locomen, too, were affected, for on the 'Q1s' the absence of running frames offered a startlingly clear view from the cab of rapidly revolving coupling rods. Again, as with Bulleid's 'Merchant Navy' 'Pacifics', cast steel coupled wheels were of the double-disc pattern. Even the running numbers, C1-C40, employed Bulleid's variation of Continental practice. None the less, the 'Q1s' were a powerful addition to SR stock. BR renumbered them 33001-40, and all lasted well into the 1960s. The prototype was set aside for the National Collection.

American-designed, and built by Vulcan, SR USA TANK No 67 served in Europe as WD No 1282 until it and 13 others were bought by the SR, late in 1946, for £2,500 each. Work at Southampton Docks then occupied the locomotive until the cessation of steam locomotion on BR's Southern Region in July 1967 brought about withdrawal. *Steamchest*

WANKERS

This none too respectful nickname was given by LB&SCR men to D.E. Marsh's Class 'I1' 4-4-2Ts, 20 of which were built at Brighton Works in 1906-07. These engines were employed on relatively unimportant tasks, where sustained periods of hard work were seldom called for. The class was improved to some extent by being rebuilt as Class 'I1X' during the late 1920s, and all but one succeeded in entering BR stock. At one time, 10 Class 'I1s' worked from Brighton and Horsham sheds; there they were more kindly known as the WEALDEN TANKS.

WARTHOGS

See FLYING PIGS and UTILITIES.

WATERBURIES

This was an ironic nickname for the GER 0-6-0s, later LNER Class 'J14', which were also known, in equally sarcastic vein, as SWIFTS (qv). These engines, sluggish in performance, were notoriously unpunctual in timekeeping. The allusion was to Waterbury, a city in New Haven, Conn, USA, which was famous at the time for its manufacture of watches. It was said, too, that a peculiar watchlike ticking sound emanated from the WATERBURIES on occasion.

Curiously, on another railway, the NER, a class of 2-4-0 gained the same nickname for exactly opposite reasons! The punctuality of the NER's Class 'G' 2-4-0s was quite above reproach. Designed by T.W. Worsdell, and built in 1887-88, these locomotives were rebuilt as 6 ft 1½ in 4-4-0s from 1900 onwards, and became Class 'D23' under LNER auspices. All 20 survived the Grouping; withdrawals began in 1929, and by 1935 the class was extinct.

WATERBURIES. NER 2-4-0 No 679, built at Darlington in December 1887, was one of 20 which were designed for passenger services on secondary lines. Highly successful, these engines put in much better annual mileages than any of T.W. Worsdell's earlier passenger types, and all were rebuilt as 4-4-0s by his brother, Wilson Worsdell, in 1900-04. *Author's Collection*

WATERCARTS
See BABY SCOTS.

WATH DAISIES
Faced with hump-shunting demands at the new marshalling yard at Wath-on-Dearne which the GCR opened in 1907, J.G. Robinson, using his highly successful 0-8-0 tender engine (see OLD LADIES) as a basic design, commissioned four massive 0-8-4Ts from Beyer Peacock & Co. Three-cylindered, and with 4 ft 8 in driving wheels, even these monsters had difficulty in starting heavy trains in bad weather. Thus, in 1929, Nigel Gresley took the daring step of fitting one, No 6171, with booster equipment. At Wath these huge locomotives were always known as WATH DAISIES, though occasionally a driver would refer humorously to his massive charge as a MICKEY MOUSE. Two more, both booster-fitted, were shopped by Gorton Works in 1932. Eventually, two survivors were replaced at Frodingham in the late 1950s

—not by diesel-electric shunters, but by ex-GNR Class 'J50' 0-6-0Ts! See also HUMPIES.

WEALDEN TANKS
See WANKERS.

WEE BENS
When Peter Drummond succeeded David Jones as HR Locomotive Superintendent in 1896 he disrupted the traditional HR pattern of o/c passenger locomotives. His first design, an i/c 4-4-0, bore a remarkable resemblance to a similar type only just introduced on the LSWR by his brother, Dugald. Eight of these HR 4-4-0s were built by Dubs & Co in 1898, and were named after Scottish mountains. Tough little engines, the 'Bens', increased latterly to 20 in number, served the HR well. In 1908, when six of a later class, with bigger boilers, entered traffic, the 4-4-0s were segregated by HR men into WEE BENS and BIG BENS. The latter were all withdrawn by June 1938, but, surprisingly, 10 of the smaller vari-

WATH DAISIES. LNER Class 'S1' 0-8-4T No 6173, seen here at Mexborough, was built by Beyer Peacock (Works No 5005) in 1908, and started life as GCR Class '8H' No 1173. The huge tank spent most of its working life at Wath and Whitemoor Yards and, never fitted with a booster, was withdrawn, as BR No 69903, in March 1954. *Steamchest*

Clearly influenced by his brother, Dugald, Peter Drummond's first design for the HR introduced the i/c 4-4-0 to that august concern. WEE BEN No 14404 *Ben Clebrig*, ready for action outside Inverness shed, was built by Dubs & Co (Works No 3692/1899) as HR No 8, and perished as BR No 54404 in October 1950. *Author's Collection*

ety lasted to enter BR stock, and February 1953 arrived ere the last WEE BEN, No 54398 *Ben Alder*, Dubs-built in 1898, was set aside for preservation. Though the loco lingered on to 1964, preservation, alas, was never effected.

WEE DRUMMONDS

In 1879, to offer a wider route availability for all classes of traffic, Dugald Drummond designed a class of 101 0-6-0 tender engines for the NBR. The WEE DRUMMONDS, as they were appreciatively known, even handled through goods trains from Glasgow to Newcastle, a distance of 175 miles, with gradients thrown in. They were equally at home handling main-line passenger trains. Classified 'J34' by the LNER, early withdrawals were heavy, however, and the last two survivors met their end in January 1928.

THE WELLAND DIVER

This was one of six Stirling 0-4-2STs which

were shopped from Doncaster Works in 1876-78. No 503 acquired its distinctive nickname on 18 July 1878, when it had the misfortune to fall into the River Welland near its home base at Stamford. Rather like the NBR's DIVER (qv), it was rescued after a while, minus chimney, and after repair it worked on until withdrawal came in June 1913.

WEMBLEYS

Of 31 0-6-0s, later LNER Class 'J9', which were built for the GCR by Neilson & Co in 1891, no fewer than 25 were sent north to Scotland in 1925. This unusual procedure was made feasible by the return further south of many ex-ROD 2-8-0s from war service abroad. The 'J9s' were none too popular on the NBR Section, and, in common with their six sisters who remained in England, all vanished by December 1936. In the Glasgow area locomen, intrigued by their GCR appearance, nicknamed them WEMBLEYS, after

Dugald Drummond's Class 'D' 5-foot 0-6-0s were held in great affection by NBR men as WEE DRUMMONDS. No 306, seen here with a full complement of cheerful supporters, was one of 96 which were built at Cowlairs between 1879 and 1883, and bears all the hallmarks of early Drummond practice. Withdrawals were heavy in early LNER days, and No 306 perished, as NBR No 1383, in June 1923. *J.F. McEwan*

the famous Exhibition then being held in London.

WEMYSS BAY PUGS

Perhaps the best of W. Pickersgill's designs for the CR, 12 heavy o/c 4-6-2Ts were constructed by NBL in 1917. They were designed to handle fast suburban trains between Glasgow and Gourock/Wemyss Bay; and, with a total water capacity of 1,800 gallons and room in their bunkers for 3 tons of coal, there was never any doubt as to their ability to cope with this demanding traffic. Their weight in working order was just over 91½ tons, and Caley men took the WEMYSS BAY PUGS, as they were known, warmly to their hearts. Most of these tanks lived to pass into BR stock, and several earned their keep latterly by banking trains up to Beattock Summit. The last, No 55359, was withdrawn in October 1953. The LMSR classified these useful tanks '4P'.

WEST END TANKS

These were six 2-4-0WTs which were designed by J.C. Craven for the LB&SCR in 1858. Built at Brighton Works, each cost £2,300, and once Victoria Station was opened they were employed on suburban passenger services. Hard rough riders, they were, however, detested by Brighton men, to whom they were known simply as BRUTES. These well tanks were also very prone to hot axle boxes. Shortly after William Stroudley's accession, the WEST END TANKS began to disappear in 1871, when No 128, the only one which had not been renewed in 2-4-0 tank form, was withdrawn. The last of the remaining five, No 378, which had been renewed as a 2-4-0 side tank in 1868, was finally discarded, with a mileage of 604,833, in January 1889.

WEST RIDING GOODS

These were 10 small-wheeled 0-6-0s which were designed specially by Patrick Stirling in 1883 to handle heavy coal trains over the steep West Riding gradients. In most other respects they were akin to the GNR's STANDARD GOODS (qv). After strenuous careers on West Riding coal traffic they were replaced by more powerful locomotives, whence the WEST RIDING GOODS reverted to light local duties. The first withdrawal took place in October 1927, but, surprisingly, No 4027 of this LNER 'J7' Class lingered on at Ardsley until September 1936.

WET STEAMERS

Following the unsuccessful debut of the GNR's 0-8-2Ts (see LONG TOM TANKS) on London suburban work, H.A. Ivatt introduced a new series of 0-6-2Ts, his class 'N1s'. Fifty-six were built at Doncaster in 1907-12, and these engines scored an immediate success. Most worked in the London area, until Gresley's Class 'N2' 0-6-2Ts, more powerful still, took over in 1920-21. Many of the 'N1s' finished up in the West Riding of Yorkshire, the bulk of them with condensing equipment removed. GNR men there invariably referred to the 'N1s' correctly enough, as WET STEAMERS—then cheerfully confounded logic by styling a few which had been superheated as SUPERHEATED WET STEAMERS! The latter were recognisable by the twin anti-vacuum valves which were sited behind the chimney.

Whatever, 55 of these hard-working 'N1' tanks entered BR service in 1948, with 24 of them still stationed in the West Riding. By 1956 the London and Home Counties allocation had shrunk to three, and No 69462, an Ardsley engine, was last to go, in April 1959. No 69461, withdrawn five years earlier, had the doubtful distinction of serving as a stationary boiler at Shoeburyness until it was cut up in March 1963. The memory, however, of an 'N1' grappling with a heavy suburban train on the Hotel Curve at King's Cross will not fade readily from the minds of those who were privileged to witness the drama.

WHIPPETS

Rivalry between the CR and the NBR in Scotland was never dull. Both had to face heavy routes to get south, and while the CR opted, in 1906, to go for such six-coupled giants as *Cardean*, etc, the NBR, remembering the severe curvature of its Aberdeen and Carlisle roads, decided to pin its faith in very powerful 'Atlantics'. Thus 20 remarkably beautiful 4-4-2 tender engines were built by NBL and R. Stephenson & Co over the years 1906-11. Their designer, W.P. Reid, broke further with Holmes's NBR tradition by lavishing stirring Scottish names on his startling new creations. Six of Reid's 'Atlantics' remained saturated at the Grouping, and became LNER Class 'C10'. The remaining 14, fitted with superheaters from 1915 onwards, were grouped, together with two new engines which were added by NBL in 1921, as LNER Class 'C11'.

Excellent steamers and brilliant hill-climbers, the NBR 'Atlantics' could still travel at speed when required. Their appetite for coal, though, placed heavy demands on train crews. Nevertheless, the more adventurous NBR men worshipped the WHIPPETS, as they were known. Withdrawals began in 1933, and No 9875, taken out of service in December 1937, then reinstated in June 1938, ultimately outlived her sisters by lasting until November 1939. Hopes that a NBR 'Atlantic' might be preserved were dashed when No 9875 *Midlothian* was, in fact, subjected to immediate demolition. But at least that engine had the consolation of finishing up with the highest class record of 1,408,823 miles.

WHITBY BOGIES
The first NER 4-4-0s with inside cylinders, 10 of these locomotives were built by R. Stephenson & Co in 1864-65. Driving wheels were 5 ft 0¹/4 in and the 4-4-0s short wheelbase bogies made them suitable for work on the sharply-curved Pickering to Whitby line. These engines had double frames and stovepipe chimneys, and, at first, only a weatherboard was provided in the way of shelter for train crews. Despite reasonable success, the life of the class was not long. Withdrawals started in 1883, and the last four were cut up in 1893.

WHITBY TANKS
See WILLIES.

WHITSTABLE CRAB
Until James Stirling arrived on the scene, the SER was badly supplied with tank shunting engines. Stirling's response was to introduce his versatile Class 'R' 0-6-0Ts, 25 of which were built at Ashford Works between 1888 and 1898; in later years 13 of them were rebuilt as Class 'R1'. The association of the Stirling tanks with the Folkestone Harbour and Canterbury & Whitstable branches was close, and, though traffic on the Whitstable branch faded in post-Second World War years, it was entirely appropriate that the last train on the branch, on 29 November 1952, should be headed by Class 'R1' No 31010— the WHITSTABLE CRAB, as it was known locally. Press, radio and television assisted that day in making the occasion a truly memorable one.

All 13 'R1s' entered BR stock, and at least half a dozen soldiered on at Folkestone Harbour, banking trains—until mid-1959, when, to the disgust of many locally, they were replaced by Western Region 0-6-0 pannier tanks. In the event, the last 'R1', No 31337, was broken up at Ashford on 7 May 1960.

WIGAN BASHERS
This was a numerous and highly versatile class of L&YR 0-6-0, first built by J.A.F. Aspinall in 1889, and perpetuated by his successors, Hoy and Hughes, right up to 1917. Some 448 of these sturdy engines were built, and all passed into LMSR stock, whence they were segregated into superheated and unsuperheated series. To their dying days they were still known affectionately as the WIGAN BASHERS. Fortunately, No 52322, an Aspinall product of 1895, was secured by a private owner when it was withdrawn in August 1960, and is now preserved. The last to go to the breakers was No 52515, in December 1962.

WIGAN PIGS
See IRONCLADS.

WILLIES
These were the first six-coupled passenger tanks on the NER. Designed by Wilson

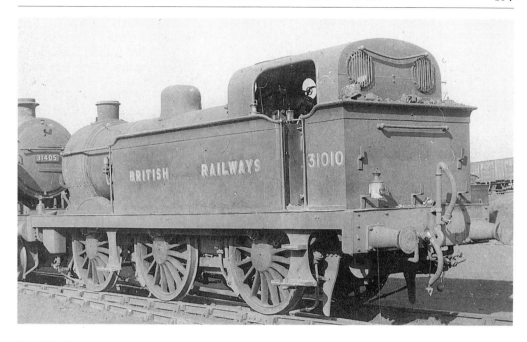

Ex-SER Class 'R1' No 31010, the WHITSTABLE CRAB, finished its career, in August 1959, with stovepipe chimney, low dome, Ross pop safety valves, and Stirling cab. *Steamchest*

Built at Horwich in December 1894 as L&YR No 270, WIGAN BASHER No 52271 looked as sturdy as ever when it was photographed at Manchester (Exchange) on 4 July 1959. Its long life came to an end two years later. *Steamchest*

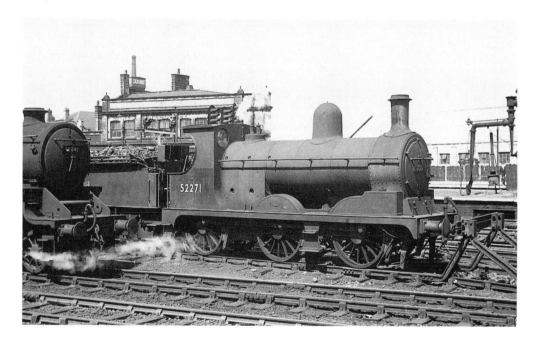

Nicknamed initially a WOOLLEY WILLY, and latterly a WHITBY TANK by virtue of its service at Whitby, ex-NER 4-6-2T No 692, the longest-lived 'A6', acquired BR No 69796 in due course. The last 18 months of its life were spent station piloting at Hull (Paragon), before withdrawal came its way in March 1953. *Author's Collection*

Worsdell, 10 were built at Gateshead Works as 4-6-0Ts in 1907-08, and, designated Class 'W', they became popularly known as WILLIES. During the First World War provision of increased coal and water capacity became a matter of extreme urgency. The WILLIES, therefore, were rebuilt as 4-6-2Ts, with extended frames and a longer bunker, after which they became known as WOOLLEY WILLIES! Rugged and coal hungry, these hard-working 'Pacific' tanks, later LNER Class 'A6', served in the Whitby and Scarborough areas for many years. Latterly they were also known as the WHITBY TANKS. The last in service, No 69796, was withdrawn from Hull (Paragon) in March 1953.

WOLVES
See METROPOLITAN TANKS.

WONDERS
Gratefully known as WONDERS by LSWR men, long inured to the idiosyncrasies of Dugald Drummond's 4-6-0s, Robert Urie's simple robust 2-cyl Class 'N15' 4-6-0s were a success immediately the first engine, No 736, entered public service in September 1918. Sixteen more were added in 1918-22, and R.E.L. Maunsell, acknowledging the usefulness of the type, contributed three more for the SR in 1923. Superheated in 1928-30, the 'N15s' had already been named in 1925, and they joined Maunsell's later, improved 'N15s' (see SCOTSMEN) in forming the famous 'King Arthur' Class. The Urie 'N15s' perished to a man in the 1950s; No 30738 of the species completed 1,460,218 miles before bowing the knee in March 1958. It had carried the name *King Pellinore*.

WOODFORD PIG
The introduction by Sir Henry Fowler in 1927 of 2-cyl suburban 2-6-4Ts laid the foundation for a lengthy development of the type by both the LMSR and BR. Stanier con-

tributed 205 taper-boilered 2-6-4Ts, Fair-bairn, his successor, 277, and BR added 155 from 1951 onwards. One of the Fairbairn LMS tanks, No 42082, known locally as the WOODFORD PIG, was stationed at Wood-ford shed for some years, until the rapid decline of the ex-GCR main line from Marylebone saw Woodford depot close in June 1965.

WOOLWORTHS

During the immediate post-First World War years, Woolwich Arsenal, anxious to allevi-ate potential unemployment amongst its skilled staff, sponsored the manufacture of 100 complete sets of parts for Maunsell's Class 'N' 2-6-0s of the SE&CR; boilers were provided by NBL of Glasgow. The SR later purchased 50 of these sets for assembly at Ashford Works, and the resultant locomo-tives were put into service in 1924-25 as Nos 826-75. Because of teething difficulties, and the nature of their origin, the engines acquired the nickname WOOLWORTHS,

while men of the SR's Eastern Region called them MONGOLIPERS. But latterly these locomotives earned themselves a fine reputa-tion, and all lasted into the 1960s. No 31874, rescued from Barry scrapyard in 1973, func-tions today on the Mid Hants Railway, bear-ing the name *Anzac*.

Other sets were bought from Woolwich Arsenal. The Metropolitan Railway bought six, from which Armstrong Whitworth assembled six 2-6-4Ts. The Great Southern Railway of Ireland took 27 sets, and created from these 20 'K1' and six 'K1A' 'Moguls'. It has also been said that Woolwich Arsenal's final 18 sets went to Roumanian State Rail-ways, who produced 12 locomotives from them.

THE WRECK

'The Wreck of the Hesperus' is a classic in seafaring annals. Colonel H.F. Stephens, with his fondness for classical allusions, used the name *Hesperus* several times on locomo-tives serving on his light railway 'empire'.

WOOLWORTH No 1828 entered traffic in 1924, after the SR had contracted to purchase 20 engines and tenders from Woolwich Arsenal for £79,600. Classified 'N', the 2-6-0 was eventually sold for scrap to P. Wood, of Queensborough, in 1964. *Steamchest*

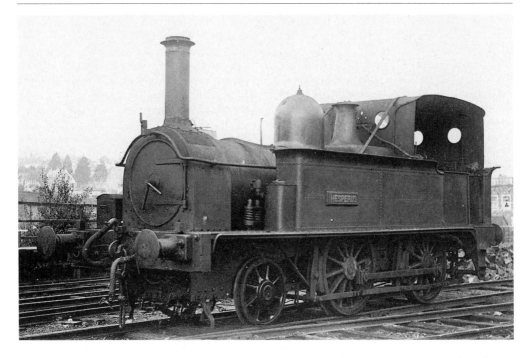

THE WRECK. WR&PR No 4 *Hesperus* led an eventful life. Built by Sharp Stewart & Co (Works No 2578/1876) for the Watlington & Princes Risborough Railway as No 2, it became GWR No 1384 seven years later, and was rebuilt at Swindon in 1899. Sold to the Bute Works Supply Co in 1911, it later served the WC&PR, and was cut up in June 1937. *Author's Collection*

Ergo, nothing was more natural than the nickname THE WRECK which Weston, Clevedon & Portishead Light Railway men bestowed upon their *Hesperus*, a third-hand Sharp Stewart 2-4-0T of elderly vintage. The little line was closed by the GWR in 1940, some time after THE WRECK itself finally foundered.

YANKEES/YANKEE MONGRELS

The first 2-6-0s and eight-wheeled tenders on the GNR were imports from the USA in 1899, the reason for such unusual procedure being that British locomotive builders were unable at the time to meet new orders. The same reason also obliged the MR and GCR to order 'Moguls' from Baldwin and Schenectady Locomotive Works. With their long chimneys, bar frames and exceptionally roomy windowed cabs, the American 2-6-0s were unmistakeable, and soon became known as YANKEES, or, on occasion, YANKEE MONGRELS. In practice they proved to be rather less powerful than the average British 0-6-0, and those on the GNR were scrapped after 10 years' use. Perhaps the general experience of all three British companies is best summed up in the words of S.W. Johnson, the MR's Locomotive Superintendent:

The foreign engines worked their trains satisfactorily, but I cannot name any points in which they showed superiority. It was the engineering strike [in England] which caused us to put our work out to America.

For the same reasons, another firm of Ameri-

Midland Railway YANKEE 2-6-0 No 2505 was supplied by the Baldwin Locomotive Works, Philadelphia, (Works No 16625) in 1899. Renumbered 2204 in 1907, the American 'Mogul' suffered early withdrawal three years later. *Author's Collection*

GWR 0-6-2T No 193 was another YANKEE. Formerly Barry Railway No 117, it was one of five which were built by the Cooke Loco & Machine Co of New Jersey in 1899, during which year British locomotive manufacturers were inundated with orders. Eventually taken into GWR stock as No 193, the loco was cut up at Swindon *circa* 1930 after a period on the Sales List. *Steamchest*

can locomotive constructors, the Cooke Loco and Machine Co of Paterson, New Jersey, also had orders from two Welsh railways. The Barry Railway imported five 0-6-2Ts in October 1899; they arrived at Barry Docks in parts, and were assembled at Barry Works. More powerful than their British counterparts, they were, however, desperately heavy on coal and water. All duly entered GWR stock, but were cut up between 1927 and 1932. The second Cooke contingent consisted of two large 0-8-2Ts for the Port Talbot Railway & Docks. Outside cylindered, they, too, were assembled at Barry Works towards the end of 1899. Rebuilt at Swindon with a taper boiler, Belpaire firebox and other GWR features, both engines were duly absorbed in 1922. They were withdrawn, in December 1928 and April 1929, with mileages, since the rebuild, of less than 350,000.

Also known as YANKEES were some 4-4-0Ts which were supplied by Dubs & Co to the HR in 1891. They were originally built for the Uruguay Eastern Railway, but delivery was never made. The HR accepted two on a year's trial, and these were placed on branch service at Burghhead. As performance proved satisfactory, the HR ordered three more, and these were delivered by Dubs in 1893. Latterly three of the five bore names. The initial pair lasted longest, but by 1934 all were withdrawn by the LMSR. When first introduced on the HR, these tanks were, somewhat confusedly, dubbed AMERICAN TANKS.

Perhaps the oldest YANKEES were three 4-2-0s, which were built by Norris & Co of Philadelphia in 1839-42 for the Birmingham & Gloucester Railway. They were eventually acquired by the Taff Vale Railway, but were all condemned, or disposed of, by 1858.

YELLOW BELLIES

A none too complimentary nickname which was often applied to L&YR tank engines. One can only assume that the term was coined, and employed, by men belonging to rival railway companies!

YORKIES

These were useful and versatile i/c 4-4-2Ts, 30 of which were supplied to the NBR by the Yorkshire Engine Co in 1911-13. Designed by W.P. Reid, they handled heavy suburban passenger traffic around Edinburgh and Glasgow for many years until Gresley 'N2' 0-6-2Ts (see TEDDY BEARS) arrived to oust them. Latterly the YORKIES were allowed to decline somewhat out of use. All lasted, however, well into the 1950s, and Nos 67474 and 67460 even held out to April 1960.

Z

ZEPPELINS

See CRABS.

INDEX OF LOCOMOTIVE TYPES